THE COOPERATIVE INDOOR & OUTDOOR GAME BOOK

• •

EASY CLASSROOM AND FIELD GAMES FOR FITNESS AND FUN

• •

by Priscilla Huff

SCHOLASTIC
PROFESSIONAL BOOKS

New York • Toronto • London • Auckland • Sydney

D1127887

• •

With thanks to my husband and sons,
and all my special students. I could
not have done it without them.

• •

No part of this publication may be reproduced in whole or in part or stored in a
retrieval system, or transmitted in any form, or by any means, electronic, mechanical,
photocopying, recording, or otherwise, without written permission of the publisher.
For information regarding permission, write to:
Scholastic Inc.
730 Broadway,
New York, NY 10003.

Designed by Design Five, New York City
Production by Design Five, New York City
Cover Design by Vincent Ceci
Cover photography by Richard Hutchings
Illustrations by Katie Jellinghaus and George Ulrich

ISBN 0-590-49180-6

TABLE OF CONTENTS

Introduction

Over the past 20 years, I have taught in both school and community physical education and recreational programs. My students ranged in age and ability, so I had ample opportunity to see which games and equipment worked and which didn't and to make any necessary adjustments.

Because several of the programs had limited budgets, I often made or adapted equipment from inexpensive materials and ordinary household items. As a result, I was able to set as a goal for my games to always have enough equipment so that everyone could play. As I adapted equipment, I also adapted games. Another goal of my games was for everyone to have the most fun possible.

Through my teaching experiences, I have found that the more a group is involved in a game, the more likely the players are to enjoy the game. Two important side benefits of their involvement and enjoyment are an increase in fitness and gross motor skills and fewer discipline problems. These games are intended as a resource to help your students develop their physical and mental potential while working cooperatively with their classmates to achieve common goals.

I hope you will enjoy using this book in addition to but not as a replacement for other physical education or recreational programs. I also hope that you and your students will be inspired to come up with new and original equipment ideas and further variations on these games.

Priscilla Huff

Using This Book With Your Class

▶ *The purpose of this book is to provide teachers of grades K–4 with an activity program that focuses on cooperative play and uses inexpensive, readily available materials. In addition, teachers of visually impaired children, students in wheelchairs, or differently abled classes will find many of these games well suited to their needs.*

In Part One, games are divided into sections according to the equipment needed. Under each game title is a list of equipment and the physical, curriculum, and cooperative skills involved in the game. The following setup includes the game formation (whether it involves partners of teams sitting in a circle, for instance) and highlights any pre-game preparation such as blowing up balloons or lining up milk carton bowling pins. Clear, concise directions follow, as well as hints for safe, smooth-running play, game variations, and adaptations for differently abled children.

Part Two features game and activities for special events. Part Three includes suggestions on where to find materials and how to adapt them to make game equipment.

▶ Getting It Going

To help you set up a successful activity program, here are some guidelines on rules, demonstrations, and game modifications.

1. When your players arrive, begin with some warm-ups to get the children moving.

2. Tell the children the name of the game, and have the players sit in playing formation.

3. Explain the object of the game and give the basic rules. Keep the rules brief. The children want to begin playing right away! Take only a few questions, assuring the players that they can ask more questions after a demonstration.

4. Point out the boundaries and any safety factors of the game—which direction to run in or how to tag by lightly tapping on another player's arm with one hand, for example.

5. Then, with the children in formation, have them start the game and play it for a few minutes. Tell them that this is just a demonstration, and you will not keep score.

6. Clarify any rules or procedures, answer any additional questions, and start the game.

7. During play, do not tolerate poor sportsmanship or over-aggressiveness. Give players a warning for a first violation and follow it, if necessary, with a period of time-out (tell the player that he or she can re-enter the game after gaining the needed self-control).

8. Since one of the objects of any game is to have fun, if play is not going smoothly, you can change the game so it *will* be fun. For example, you might try the following:
    - Mix up the teams if one constantly dominates the other(s).
    - Create smaller teams and rotate them frequently to allow for more participation.
    - Enlarge or reduce boundaries if players need more or less space.
    - Be ready to substitute another similar game if this one is causing too many problems, such as fighting or repeated injuries, and remember that this can happen to even the best teacher!
    - Modify the rules so everyone has a chance to participate.
    - See other suggestions in Playing Cooperatively.
9. Stop the game at the height of interest so children will want to come back to it again.
10. Alternate active and quiet games during the playing time and end with a cooling-down period and a quiet game.
11. At the end of playing time, ask players what they did or did not like about the game so that next time it can go even more smoothly.

▶ Setting Up

These are some tips on establishing playing boundaries and using equipment.

1. Make the size of your playing area appropriate to the age of your players.
2. Know your area or field before you play a game. Clearly mark boundaries and any hazards that cannot be moved or changed. To familiarize players with game lines, have them walk or jog around boundary markers.
3. When playing outdoors, have action run parallel to any nearby roads to avoid having children run into the street.
4. Try not to have any players looking directly into the sun.
5. To ensure maximum participation, have enough equipment (and some extras) for all players.
6. Have the equipment ready to hand out so there won't be any delay in getting the game started.
7. Designate helpers to assist in handing out and collecting equipment (children are eager to do this until they reach junior high).
8. Make sure the children do not use the equipment inappropriately or needlessly destroy it.

▶ Playing Cooperatively

Most children need practice in learning to play cooperatively. They are more used to competitive games that emphasize high scores, penalties, and winning. Cooperative play, on the other hand, emphasizes teamwork, good sportsmanship, and skill improvement. To encourage cooperation among your students, here is a list of ways to make all games less competitive and more cooperative.

1. **Equal Turns:** Have all team members take one turn (at bat, to receive a pass, etc.) before any player takes two. Make sure all players try a practice round before scoring begins.
2. **Teamwork:** Have teams compete to improve their time or to better their previous scores instead of competing against one another.
3. **Position Rotation:** After a certain amount of playing time, have players change to a new position until everyone has had the chance to play all the positions.
4. **No "Outs":** Instead of having a player who is "out" leave the game, assign a "fun" penalty. A player can also go to another team or group.
5. **More Equipment:** To increase participation and action, play a game with more than one ball (or other equipment) whenever possible.
6. **Points:** Give points to a team for good sportsmanship or special effort.
7. **Double or Nothing:** In a game whose winner scores the best of 3 rounds, play the last round "double or nothing" to give the losing team the chance to even the score.
8. **Unlimited Fouls:** In games that involve striking a ball, have the players try until they successfully hit or kick the ball into fair territory.
9. **Play Backwards:** To lessen the intensity or competitiveness of a game, play it backwards. For example, have players bat with their opposite hands and run to third base instead of first.
10. **Choosing Teams:** To avoid hurt feelings, be creative in assigning players to teams. For example,
    - The leader can ask the players to pick team names and decide which team they want to be on. If the teams are uneven, volunteers can go to another team, or players can have more than one turn.
    - Put all the boys' names in one hat and all the girls' names in another. The leader takes turns drawing out one girl's name and one boy's name for each team.
    - Let the players decide a fair way to choose teams, but discourage them from using a system that involves picking in front of others because it hurts to be chosen last.
    - Divide the class into teams by the color of the children's sneakers or shirts; use birthdays or the first letter of their last name.
    - Count off by numbers (primary children may have trouble remembering their numbers).

▶ *Safety First!*

As with all classroom activities, it's critical to ensure the safety of your students. Here are some important reminders before you begin playing.

- Check that the playing area is free of debris, holes, or uneven surfaces. Make sure there is enough space to play the game. (If not, consider alternating smaller teams, or modify the game rules to safely accommodate the space.)

- To prevent possible injuries, check your equipment for cracks, splits, tears, or other damage. Have extra materials on hand.
- If you're playing outdoors, pay attention to weather conditions that can limit visibility or make footing difficult. *Never* consider playing outside if there is the possibility of lightning. Because of abrasions and other injuries that can occur when children fall, use blacktop (macadam) or cement playing areas only when no other areas are available.
- Keep starting lines, turning points, and finish lines away from walls, poles, and other obstacles. Avoid accidents by having children stop on a line rather than use a permanent structure to stop themselves. Avoid collisions and tripping by using markers such as plastic milk cartons or cardboard boxes for players to run around.
- Avoid games with purposeful body contact. Although children will occasionally bump into one another, avoid games whose objective is to have players push or shove. Children tend to go overboard when given permission to use physical contact. Be prepared to stop a game if play becomes overly aggressive. Remember that it takes time to teach children to play cooperatively. (Later, analyze the game to see if it was inappropriate for the age or maturity level of that particular class, or if the game itself was too combative.)
- Make sure the game is appropriate for the age and maturity level of the children. For example, some games may require more stamina or a higher skill level than younger children may have. Try to have children of the same age compete against one another. If the group includes children of varying ages, divide the number of older children equally among the teams.
- Before physically active games, have players warm up with stretching and other preliminary exercises to prevent pulled muscles or other injuries. Take time to have players cool down, especially after strenuous games. Provide frequent water breaks during hot weather.
- Check whether any students have health conditions that restrict their participation. Most children with asthma, allergies, diabetes, epilepsy, and other health conditions can enjoy playing without any problem. Know specific procedures to follow in case of emergency.
- You should know basic first aid procedures and have emergency numbers (and a phone) readily available. A first aid kit and ice packs should be part of your basic equipment. No matter how safety conscious you may be, injuries can occur. Be prepared!
- Above all, use your common sense while you enjoy these games with your students!

Resources

● ●

▶ *For more information on physical activities for children, you can call or write to the following organizations:*

The President's Council on Physical Fitness and Sports
701 Pennsylvania Avenue, NW
Suite 250
Washington, DC 20004
(202) 272–3430

American Alliance for Health, Physical Education,
Recreation and Dance (AAHPERD)
1900 Association Drive
Reston, VA 22091
(703) 476–3400

Letter to Parents

• •

▶ *You can make copies of this letter to hand out to your students during the first week of school. You can save time and paper by highlighting the objects you need for a particular activity. Remind your students to return the letter with the materials from home. Place the letters in a file until you're ready to send them home again. If you don't write any names on the letters, you can redistribute them.*

Dear Parent:

We need your help!

Our class needs the following items for our cooperative games and activities. Please start saving them now, and I'll let you know when we'll need them.

1. tubes from paper towels, gift wrap, kitchen wrap
2. large bed sheets
3. tires, hoops
4. cans from soup, juice, tuna fish, etc.
5. pieces of cloth, fabric scraps
6. tennis balls, beach balls, balloons
7. cardboard sheets and boxes
8. clothesline, rope, yarn
9. paper plates, construction paper, crepe paper
10. bottle caps, checkers
11. plastic gallon containers
12. other:

Thanks,

Games That Use Simple Materials

Games That Use Beanbags

These games emphasize a variety of physical skills, including underhand tossing, overhand throwing, jumping, and tagging. The games stress teamwork and partner skills and include suggestions for younger children. You may want to look at the section Games That Use Balls and Balloons. You can often substitute beanbags for the balls in those games.

When games call for music, you may want to use a tape or cassette player, radio, or even live piano or guitar music.

Beanbag Pitch

▶ **Equipment:** Beanbags, target
▶ **Skills:** Throwing (overhand), tossing (underhand)
▶ **Setup:** Teams of 3-4 players. To make targets see directions in Part Three, Making and Adapting Equipment.
▶ **Directions:** Players take turns tossing or throwing beanbags at the target or through its openings. Each player has 1-3 tosses or throws.
▶ **Scoring:** 1 point for each beanbag that hits the target or goes into one of the holes. If a beanbag lands halfway into a hole, the player can throw it again.
▶ **Hints:** Younger children find it easier to toss rather than throw the beanbags. Enlarge target openings for younger children and allow them to stand closer to the target.
▶ **Variations: 1.** Play Tick, Tack, Toe, tossing or throwing 3 beanbags into 3 holes in a row or on a diagonal. **2.** See how far away players can get from the target and still hit the target.
▶ **Adaptations:** Children in wheelchairs need another child to assist them or a way to retrieve thrown beanbags. They may also need to move closer to the target.

Beanbag Toss

- **Equipment:** 1 "jack" beanbag (designate any beanbag, preferably in a bright color), beanbags for each team
- **Skills:** Tossing (underhand); partner skills; teamwork
- **Setup:** Teams of 2 or more players in lines
- **Directions:** This game is similar to the Italian bowling game, bocci. One player tosses the "jack" beanbag from behind a line to the end of the playing space. Each team then takes turns trying to toss its beanbags closest to the jack.
- **Scoring:** 2 points for each beanbag that lands on or touches the jack, 1 point for each beanbag that lands within 6 inches of the jack. 11 or 15 points constitutes a game; a match consists of 2 out of 3 games.
- **Hint:** It is easier to keep score if each team has beanbags of one color.
- **Variations: 1.** Challenge players to toss beanbags using their opposite hands. **2.** Challenge the children to stand sideways and toss the beanbags over their heads or stand with their backs to the jack and toss the beanbags over their shoulders.
- **Adaptation:** Children in wheelchairs need help to retrieve thrown beanbags.

Beanbag Team Toss

- **Equipment:** Beanbags for each player, circle targets (bicycle tires, tubes, hoops, or circles of rope or tape)
- **Skills:** Tossing (underhand), catching; teamwork
- **Setup:** 2 teams scattered on either side of a dividing ring line on the floor or playing surface; an equal number of targets scattered on both sides
- **Directions:** At the signal, each team tries to toss its beanbags into the other team's tires. Players try to stop the beanbags by catching them. At the end of 30 seconds, the leader blows a whistle and counts the total number of beanbags that are inside the targets. Play 2 more rounds. The winning team has the most accurate tosses in 2 out of 3 rounds.
- **Scoring:** 1 point for each direct hit. Players can pick up beanbags that land halfway into the targets and toss them again. Players can also pick up beanbags that miss the targets and try again.
- **Hints: 1.** Subtract points if anyone is hit in the face. **2.** Encourage players to take turns being tossers and catchers.
- **Adaptation:** Children in wheelchairs need a designated player to assist them in retrieving beanbags.

Beanbag Math

▶ **Equipment:** Beanbags, large sheet of cardboard, pencils and papers to keep score

▶ **Skills:** Tossing (underhand); problem-solving; addition, subtraction, or multiplication

▶ **Setup:** Players standing in a line; a large sheet of cardboard divided into squares in which you have written age-appropriate addition, subtraction, or multiplication problems

▶ **Directions:** Players stand 15 feet away from the cardboard and toss beanbags onto the squares. Each player in turn does a math problem out loud. The correct answer is the player's score. If the answer is not correct, the next player in line can try the problem. At the end of the game, the player(s) with the highest score wins.

▶ **Hint:** Use beanbags of different colors so the children can identify their beanbags.

5 +3	6 −4	2 +4	3 −2
8 −5	2 +2	4 −4	9 +8
4 +3	7 −2	10 −8	3 +3
4 +4	6 −3	1 +4	7 −7

Beanbag Math

• •

Beanbag Word Match

▶ **Equipment:** Large sheet of cardboard, word cards, beanbags

▶ **Skills:** Tossing (underhand); matching words

▶ **Setup:** Divide a large sheet of cardboard into squares in which you have pasted pictures of vocabulary or spelling words. Print each word on a separate card.

▶ **Directions:** Place the word cards on a nearby table or desk. Have players stand on a masking-tape line and toss a beanbag onto a picture. Players then try to select the word card that matches the picture.

▶ **Hint:** This is a good game for kindergarten students, beginning readers, and children who need practice in reading or spelling.

Beanbag Word Match

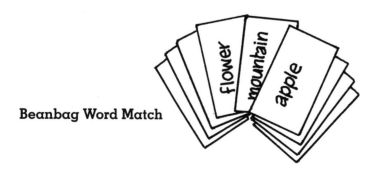
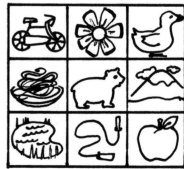

Beanbag Initials

▶ **Equipment:** Beanbag
▶ **Skills:** Tossing (underhand); knowledge of initial letters
▶ **Setup:** Players scattered throughout playing area; one player designated as It
▶ **Directions:** The player who is "It" has the beanbag. At the Go! signal, all the other players scatter around the playing area. It tries to toss the beanbag at the shoes of another player. When It has hit a player's shoes, he or she yells "Freeze!" and all the players stop. It calls out a letter of the alphabet, and the player has 15 seconds to think of 5 words that begin with that letter. If the player runs out of time, he or she becomes It. If the player does think of 5 words, then It plays another round.
▶ **Hint:** Make sure all players stop when It yells "Freeze!"
▶ **Variation:** For more advanced students, designate that only nouns (or verbs or adjectives) be used when a letter is called.

Beanbag Basketball

▶ **Equipment:** 2 wastebaskets set on chairs; 4 beanbags, 2 of each color
▶ **Skills:** Tossing (underhand), throwing (overhand), catching, passing; teamwork
▶ **Setup:** Divide the class into 2 teams, half of each team scattered on either side of the playing area. Place a basket at each end of the playing area.
▶ **Directions:** Play starts at the center line as each team throws, tosses, or passes the 2 beanbags among each of its players. After each player has had a turn, team members can try to toss the beanbags into their basket. No player can be closer than 6 feet from a basket and no player who is holding a beanbag can move his or her feet. Players from the opposing team try to prevent baskets by catching the beanbags.
▶ **Scoring:** The first team to get both beanbags in its basket gets 1 point. The first quarter ends, and play starts again from the center. If any player touches another player, it counts as a foul. The fouled player gets a free throw to the team's basket from where he or she is standing.
▶ **Hint:** Players should be no closer than 3 feet from a teammate or opponent.
▶ **Adaptation:** Students in wheelchairs can easily participate in this game.

Musical Beanbags

▶ **Equipment:** Beanbags for every other player, music
▶ **Skills:** Passing; taking turns
▶ **Setup:** Players seated in a circle
▶ **Directions:** When the music starts, the players hand the beanbags to the players on their left. . . When the music stops, the players who are holding beanbags must do a penalty (sing a phrase of a song, recite a tongue twister, etc.).
▶ **Variation:** Play the game the same way, but have the players who are *not* holding the beanbags when the music stops do a penalty.

Beanbag Cat and Rat Circle Chase

▶ **Equipment:** 2–3 beanbags of different colors
▶ **Skills:** Passing; taking turns
▶ **Setup:** Players seated in a circle
▶ **Directions:** To begin play, the leader hands a beanbag "rat" to one player and a beanbag "cat" to another player several players away. At the signal from the leader, the players pass the cat and rat beanbags around the circle in the same direction, with the cat trying to catch the rat. Each player must pass the cat and rat around in turn without skipping anyone. The cat chases the rat until the rat reaches home, the player who first started passing the rat. If the cat catches the rat, the player holding the rat has to do a penalty (sing a song, do 5 pushups, etc.) For subsequent rounds, the leader picks new players to hold the cat and rat.
▶ **Variation:** Add a third beanbag to be the dog that chases the cat that continues to chase the rat.
▶ **Adaptation:** Players can sit in chairs to be the same height as any players in wheelchairs.

Hot Beanbag Pass

▶ **Equipment:** 4–5 beanbags
▶ **Skills:** Passing, tagging; taking turns
▶ **Setup:** Players seated in a circle
▶ **Directions:** Have players sit in a circle with their legs crossed. One person stands in the middle. Give several beanbags to designated players around the circle. At the signal from the leader, players pass the beanbags in one direction around the circle. At the same time, the player in the middle tries to tag any player who is passing a beanbag. A player who is tagged while holding a beanbag becomes the tagger in the middle, and the tagger takes his or her place.
▶ **Variations: 1.** Add more beanbags or taggers to give the game more action. **2.** Make 2 or more circles if the class is large. **3.** Use balls or brooms instead of beanbags.
▶ **Adaptation:** Have players sit on chairs so that everyone is on the same level as children in wheelchairs.

Beanbag Relay

▶ **Equipment:** 2–3 beanbags for each player, 3 large trash bags
▶ **Skills:** Locomotor movements (running, walking, etc.); teamwork
▶ **Setup:** 2 teams lined up behind a starting line
▶ **Directions:** In front of each team, place an open trash bag. At the far end of the playing area, place the beanbags in an open trash bag. At the signal, the first person on each team walks (or runs, hops, jumps, etc.) toward the bag of beanbags. The players grab 1 bean bag each and return to their team, using the same locomotor movement. The players place the beanbag in their team bag and go to the end of the line while the second player goes to retrieve another beanbag. Play continues until all the beanbags have been put into the 2 team bags.
▶ **Scoring:** Each team counts its beanbags. The team with fewer beanbags has to do a penalty chosen by the other team. (2 fewer beanbags might mean 2 verses of "Mary Had a Little Lamb," 3 fewer might be 3 pushups, and so on.)
▶ **Hints: 1.** Divide the class into smaller teams for more action. **2.** Make sure the penalties are appropriate.

Jump the Alligator

▶ **Equipment:** An "alligator": 2 beanbags tied together with a length of clothesline

▶ **Skills:** Jumping

▶ **Setup:** Players standing in a circle with the leader in the center holding the alligator

▶ **Directions:** Slowly, the leader swings the alligator around the circle close to the feet of the players. The players try to jump over the alligator each time it circles. If the alligator "bites" a student's shoe or if the student does not jump in time, he or she takes one step back out of the circle. After the alligator makes a complete circle, the student steps back into the circle.

▶ **Hints: 1.** Make sure the circle is large enough to allow each student to jump and land safely. **2.** Because children in grades K–1 may have difficulty jumping over the alligator, the leader should turn the rope more slowly. The leader should have the alligator just touch the tips of the players' shoes. As the alligator comes around, players still jump to get their shoes out of the way, but avoid possible tripping.

▶ **Adaptations: 1.** Give visually impaired students a verbal cue when to jump. **2.** Students in wheelchairs can try to roll out of the way.

Beanbag Challenge

▶ **Equipment:** 1 beanbag for each player
▶ **Skills:** Tossing (underhand), throwing (overhand), catching; self-testing, partner skills
▶ **Setup:** Players scattered throughout the playing area
▶ **Directions:** With each player holding a beanbag, the leader challenges the players by asking the following questions:
  • Who can throw the beanbag up with 2 hands and catch it with 2 hands?
  • Who can throw the beanbag up with 1 hand and catch it with 1 hand?
  • Who can throw the beanbag up, clap once, and catch it?
  • Who can throw the beanbag up, clap twice, and catch it?
  • Who can throw the beanbag up, clap how many times, and catch it?
  • Who can throw the beanbag under his or her leg and catch it?
  • Who can throw the beanbag up and "catch" it on his or her back?
  • Who can put the beanbag on his or her head and sit down without it falling off?
  • Who can sit on the floor, pick up the beanbag with his or her feet, throw it up into the air and catch it?
  • Who can make up a trick catch with a beanbag? (Have half the group sit and watch the others. Members of the audience ask them which stunts they liked and why. Repeat with the other half.)
▶ **Hints: 1.** Encourage the children to be creative with their beanbag stunts. **2.** Make sure there is enough space for tossing and throwing. **3.** Discourage wild throwing by taking children's beanbags and giving them an "invisible" beanbag instead. Tell the children to let you know when they are ready to use a real beanbag again.
▶ **Variations: 1.** The list of "Who can's" is limited only by the children's imaginations! See also Paper Tube Challenge for other ideas. **2.** Do the same stunts with a partner.
▶ **Adaptation:** Differently abled children can do most of these self-testing skills.

Games That Use Milk Cartons and Plastic Bottles

• •

These games use milk cartons or plastic bottles from milk, bleach, or detergent as bowling pins, markers, balls, and catchers. Several games require whole cartons or bottles, some weighted for stability with sand, pebbles, or water. Other games use bottles that have been cut down to serve as catchers (see Making and Adapting Equipment, Part III). You may want to alert parents to save empty cartons and bottles for your class.

Milk Carton Bowling
• •

▶ **Equipment:** Weighted milk cartons, ball
▶ **Skills:** Rolling; partner skills
▶ **Setup:** Milk carton "bowling pins" in traditional triangle formation, partners in lines to bowl
▶ **Directions:** From behind a masking-tape line, partners take turns seeing how many cartons they can knock down on 2 rolls. Then the two players go to the end of the line and let the next pair bowl. Each pair of bowlers tries to better the score each turn.
▶ **Hint:** Set up several groups of cartons so more players can bowl at the same time.
▶ **Variations: 1.** Players turn their backs to the pins and roll the ball between their legs. **2.** Challenge players to bowl with their opposite hands. **3.** Increase or decrease the number of plastic cartons to make the game harder or easier. **4.** Stand rectangular cardboard boxes on end as pins.
▶ **Adaptations: 1.** Use a ball that players in wheelchairs can roll with one hand. They should take turns bowling with either hand to balance muscle use on both sides of body. **2.** Students with poor coordination can roll the ball through large tubes.

Milk Carton Dodging

▶ **Equipment:** Weighted milk carton for each child, drum
▶ **Skills:** Controlled running or walking, dodging, tagging; partner skills
▶ **Setup:** Scatter milk cartons around the playing area and have each player stand by one. As the leader beats out a rhythm on the drum, players move around the area to the beat. The objective is to dodge around the cartons without knocking any over or bumping into another player. Players can take turns being the leader.
▶ **Hints: 1.** Increase the difficulty of dodging by moving the cartons closer together. **2.** This game also familiarizes younger children with the terms *fast* and *slow*.
▶ **Variations: 1.** Have the students play Follow the Leader. **2.** Have players choose partners and shadow one another in dodging. **3.** Have students play tag using dodging.
▶ **Adaptations: 1.** Visually impaired students can put one hand on a partner's shoulder and follow him or her. **2.** Place cartons far enough apart for students to maneuver wheelchairs.

• •

Clothespin Drop

▶ **Equipment:** Plastic bottles, clothespins, numbered slips of paper
▶ **Skills:** Dropping, eye-hand coordination; partner skills
▶ **Setup:** Write a series of numbers on slips of paper. Repeat each number twice. Put slips in a box and have players choose partners by matching numbers.
▶ **Directions:** Give each pair a bottle and 10 clothespins. See which pair can drop the most clothespins into the bottles from a standing position in 5 minutes.
▶ **Variation:** Use pennies instead of clothespins.
▶ **Adaptation:** For younger children, or those with poor coordination, cut a larger hole in the top of the bottle.

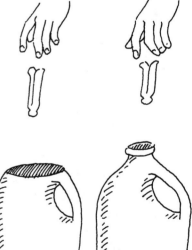

Knock Down the Bottle

- ▶ **Equipment:** 1 lightly weighted plastic bottle for every 2 players, 2 yarn or tennis balls
- ▶ **Skills:** Tossing (underhand); taking turns, partner skills
- ▶ **Setup:** Pairs stand facing one another with a bottle equidistant between them
- ▶ **Directions:** On the count of 3, both players toss the ball at the bottle and try to knock it down. If both players miss, each stands where the other player's ball has landed and tries again to knock the bottle over. See who can get 5 knockdowns first.
- ▶ **Hint:** Discourage players from purposely making wild tosses so their opponents are too far away to hit the bottle.
- ▶ **Variation:** Have pairs work in teams to knock down 2 bottles.
- ▶ **Adaptation:** Shorten the distances for players who cannot throw well.

Team Knockdown

- ▶ **Equipment:** Plastic bottles in 2 different colors, enough for every player, 1 yarn or tennis ball for each player, 1 plastic bottle "catcher" for each player
- ▶ **Skills:** Tossing (underhand); teamwork
- ▶ **Setup:** Line up the plastic bottles about 1 foot apart, alternating colors. 2 teams facing one another on either side of the lined-up bottles.
- ▶ **Directions:** Assign one set of colored bottles to each team. At the signal, the teams use their catchers to toss the balls at the opposite team's bottles.
- ▶ **Scoring:** 1 point for the first team to knock down the other team's bottles. The winner scores best out of 3 rounds.
- ▶ **Variation:** Play as above, but the first team to knock down its own bottles scores 1 point.

Guard the Bottle

▶ **Equipment:** 3 plastic bottles, 3 "catchers," balls for all players less 3
▶ **Skills:** Throwing (overhand), catching, blocking; teamwork
▶ **Setup:** Divide the class into teams of 3. Each team takes a turn standing next to 3 plastic bottles in the middle of a circle of the other players.
▶ **Directions:** Players in the circle throw balls at the bottles to knock them over. The team in the middle has 30 seconds to guard the bottles by blocking or catching the balls.
▶ **Scoring:** The score is the number of bottles, if any, left standing when time is up.
▶ **Hint:** If class is large, have 2 or more circles going at the same time.

• •

Ball Toss

▶ **Equipment:** 1 plastic bottle "catcher" for each player, 1 yarn or tennis ball for each pair
▶ **Skills:** Tossing (underhand), catching; partner skills
▶ **Setup:** Partners scattered throughout the playing area. To make catchers, see directions in Part Three, Making and Adapting Equipment.
▶ **Directions:** Partners see how many tosses they can make to one another in 1 minute.
▶ **Variations: 1.** Partners toss the ball back and forth, taking a step backwards each time. The object is to stand as far apart as possible and still complete a catch. **2.** Players stand in the circle, each holding a catcher. One player stands in the middle, holding a catcher and a ball. The player in the middle tosses the ball into the air and calls out a name. The player who is called tries to catch the ball. If the player succeeds, he or she goes into the middle. If he or she misses, the player in the middle calls out another name.

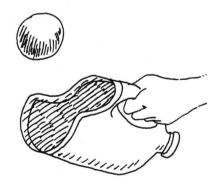

Team Cleanup

▶ **Equipment:** 1 "catcher" and yarn or tennis ball for each player, volleyball net or rope

▶ **Skills:** Throwing (overhand), catching; teamwork

▶ **Setup:** 2 teams facing one another on either side of a volleyball net or a rope draped over two chairs

▶ **Directions:** On the signal, players throw the balls over the net and try to catch those being thrown by the opposing team. Player can pick up balls that fall on the floor and throw them again. Play stops when the leader calls "freeze." Each team counts the balls on its side of the net—either on the floor or in the players' catchers.

▶ **Scoring:** The team that cleaned up its side (has the fewest balls) scores 1 point. The winning team scores the best out of 3 rounds.

▶ **Adaptations: 1.** Have a student help children in wheelchairs retrieve balls.
  2. Lower the net if necessary.

• •

Soccer Drill

▶ **Equipment:** 1 milk carton "soccer ball" for each team

▶ **Skills:** Kicking, dribbling; teamwork

▶ **Setup:** Teams of 4–5 players arranged throughout the playing area

▶ **Directions:** Demonstrate for the class how to kick the soccer ball and dribble it. Let the teams practice dribbling, lightly tapping the ball with alternating feet.

Games That Use Paper

The games in this section use a variety of paper products, including paper plates, paper tubes, crepe paper, construction paper, and cardboard. In addition to motor skills and cooperative skills, many of these games also develop curriculum skills—recognition of colors, understanding opposites, and knowledge of alphabetical order, for example.

Paper Plate Alphabet Search

▶ **Equipment:** 1 set of 26 paper plates with the letters of the alphabet written on them for each team
▶ **Skills:** Knowledge of the order of the alphabet; teamwork
▶ **Setup:** Divide class into teams and scatter the sets of alphabet plates around the playing area.
▶ **Directions:** Teams see how long it takes to gather all the alphabet letters, one at a time, and place them in order. Teams try to improve their time with each round.
▶ **Hint:** Group teams heterogeneously so that children can learn from one another. Encourage all children to search for the letters.
▶ **Variations: 1.** Have teams place the letters of the alphabet in backwards order. **2.** Spelling List Search: Give each team one of the class's weekly spelling words and have the group work together to find the letters to spell the word correctly. **3.** Vocabulary Word Search: Give each team the definition of one of the words from the class's weekly vocabulary list. Have the group work together to spell the word that matches the definition.
▶ **Adaptations: 1.** Paste copies of the sign language alphabet on paper plates to teach hearing or hearing-impaired children this alphabet. **2.** Punch braille letters into the plates with the letters written on them so visually impaired children can participate. Make sure the playing area is free from obstructions.

Paper Plate Ringers

▶ **Equipment:** 5 paper ringers, chair turned upside down on a desk
▶ **Skills:** Tossing; teamwork
▶ **Setup:** Partners or teams in lines. To make ringers, see directtions in Part Three, Making and Adapting Equipment.
▶ **Directions:** Standing behind a masking-tape line, each player tries to toss 5 paper plate rings onto the legs of an upturned chair. Players try to improve their score each round.
▶ **Variation:** Use rope or clothesline rings instead of paper plates.

Paper Plate Primary Color Search

▶ **Equipment:** Equal numbers of red, yellow, and blue paper plates
▶ **Skills:** Recognizing colors; teamwork
▶ **Setup:** 3 teams
▶ **Directions:** The leader scatters the paper plates around the playing area and gives each team either a blue, red, or yellow slip. At the signal, each team gathers and stacks the colored plates that match its slip. During subsequent rounds, teams try to improve their time.
▶ **Variation:** For second or third graders, give each team a slip in a color that is combination of two primary colors: orange (red/yellow) green (blue/yellow), purple (red/blue).

Paper Plate and Marble Race

▶ **Equipment:** Shallow paper plate and 5 marbles for each team
▶ **Skills:** Balancing; teamwork
▶ **Setup:** 4–6 teams, lined up one behind the other
▶ **Directions:** At the signal, the first person on each team takes a plate with 5 marbles on it and passes it through his or her legs to the person behind who passes it back, and so on. If any of the marbles drop off the plate, the player must replace them before continuing to pass the plate.

• •

Paper Plate Flying Discs

▶ **Equipment:** 3 flying disks, tape measure, beanbags
▶ **Skills:** Throwing a disk; taking turns
▶ **Setup:** To make flying disks, see directions in Part Three, Making and Adapting Equipment.
▶ **Directions:** Each player has 3 tries to see how far he or she can throw the disks. Measure the distance from a masking-tape starting line to where the disk lands, and mark the spot with a beanbag. Mark only the best throw of each player. Players try to better their throws with each round.

Flying Disk Golf

▶ **Equipment:** 9 plastic hoops, 1 flying disk for each player
▶ **Skills:** Throwing a disk; taking turns
▶ **Setup:** Scatter the plastic hoops throughout the playing area (or use tape to indicate "holes"). To make flying disks, see directions in Part Three, Making and Adapting Equipment.
▶ **Directions:** Players try to throw a disk into all 9 holes. If they miss a hole, players can throw the disk again from where it landed. As in golf, players keep a total of the number of tries it takes to get the disk into all 9 holes.

Paper Tube Capitals

▶ **Equipment:** 1–2 paper tubes for each player
▶ **Skills:** Knowledge of capital letters; teamwork
▶ **Setup:** Students organized into groups of 4–6
▶ **Directions:** As the leaders call out a letter, children team up to form that letter using their tubes.
▶ **Hint:** Call out letters with straight sides (A, E, F, H, etc.).

Paper Tube Hummer

▶ **Equipment:** 1 hummer for each child
▶ **Skills:** Recognizing songs; teamwork
▶ **Setup:** Teams, all players with hummers. To make hummers, see directions in Part Three, Making and Adapting Equipment.
▶ **Directions:** Have each team secretly pick a familiar tune. Have team members play it on their hummers and see if the other teams can guess the title.
▶ **Variation:** Play a favorite tape of the class and have students accompany the music on their hummers while sitting or marching around the room.

Paper Tube Rhythms

▶ **Equipment:** 1 paper tube for each student, music (optional)
▶ **Skills:** Imitating a rhythmic pattern; partner skills
▶ **Setup:** Players in pairs or threes
▶ **Directions:** Each group beats out a simple rhythmic pattern with the tubes, with or without music, and challenges the other groups to imitate it.
▶ **Variations: 1.** Follow That Leader: Players hold a paper tube in each hand and line up behind the leader. They follow the leader's movements with the tubes as they parade around the playing area. At the signal, the leader goes to the end of the line and the next person becomes the new leader.
2. Can You Be a... : The leader challenges the players to pretend to be various people, things, or animals, using their paper tubes as props. For example: an anteater, a police officer direcing traffic, or a windmill.
3. Partner Rhyming Tubes: 2 players sit on the floor across from one another with their legs crossed. Players hold a tube in each hand, vertically. To a familiar clapping rhyme such as "Peas Porridge Hot" or nursery rhyme, players tap their tubes together instead of their hands.
4. Concert Conductors: Play different classical pieces and have players move their baton tubes to the music as though they were conducting. Groups of players can also use their tubes to represent different orchestra sections, such as strings, brass, or percussion.

Paper Tube Challenge

▶ **Equipment:** 1 long paper tube (from wrapping paper) for each student
▶ **Skills:** Balancing; self-testing; partner skills
▶ **Setup:** Players scattered throughout the playing area
▶ **Directions:** With each player holding a paper tube, the leader challenges the players by asking the following questions:
  • Who can hold the paper tube with 2 hands and touch his or her head, chest, waist, knees, and toes without bending the knees? (Sing the movement song "Head, Shoulders, Knees, and Toes.")
  • Who can hold the tube with both hands and not let go as he or she steps back and forth over the tube?
  • Who can hold the tube with both hands and bring it over his or her head, behind the back, and to the front again?
  • Who can balance the tube on some part of his or her body?
  • Who can balance the tube while sitting (while kneeling?) and come back to a standing position?
  • Who can toss the tube from hand to hand without dropping it? Slowly? Fast?
  • Who can toss the tube up with 1 hand and catch it with 2 hands? With 1 hand?
  • Who can make up a new trick with the tube?
  • Who can work with 1–2 other players and make up a trick together?
▶ **Variations: 1.** See also Beanbag Challenge for other ideas. **2.** Use brooms instead of paper tubes.

Musical Streamers

▶ **Equipment:** 2 crepe paper streamers, 36–45 inches long, for each player; music

▶ **Skills:** Basic movements; knowledge of shapes

▶ **Setup:** Players scattered throughout the playing area

▶ **Directions:** The leader stands in front of the group and calls out movements to do with the streamers to the beat of the music. If the leader says to make a circle with the streamers, for example, players can move their arms in any way they choose to make circles—above their heads, at their sides, etc. At the signal, another leader takes a turn.

▶ **Variations: 1.** Make a Shape: Players make shapes with the streamers while moving in different ways around the playing area. **2.** What Is It?: Divide the class into small groups and have each group illustrate with the streamers something the other groups have to guess. Examples: a waterfall, a stream, trees blowing in the wind, a washing machine. **3.** Paper "Streams": Have the players lay their streamers horizontally on the floor around the room. Then have them step over and around the streamers, doing different movements: jumping, leaping, hopping, etc. **4.** Use square or rectangular scarves instead of crepe paper streamers, and play as above.

Jump the Candles

▶ **Equipment:** Sheets of construction paper folded in half, masking tape
▶ **Skills:** Jumping
▶ **Setup:** Stand the sheets of folded construction paper around the playing area. Secure each side to the floor with a small piece of tape.
▶ **Directions:** Have the children stand behind the folded papers and tell them to pretend these are candles. Along with the leader, have them say this nursery rhyme:

> *Jack, be nimble,*
> *Jack, be quick,*
> *Jack, jump over the candlestick.*

Players say the rhyme as they jump over the candles. If anyone jumps on a candle, he or she sets up a new one.
▶ **Hints:** Because this game can be tiring, you may want to split the class in half and have one group jump while the other sits on the side and says the rhyme 5 times for the jumpers. The object is to see which team can be first to have all members successfully jump over the candles.
▶ **Variation:** Older children can jump backwards over the candles. (For safety, have the children jump on the balls of their feet and lean slightly forward.)

• •

Paper Sailplanes

▶ **Equipment:** Large-sized construction paper, at least 8-1/2 x 14 inches, paper clips
▶ **Skills:** Throwing; teamwork
▶ **Setup:** Players in pairs or small groups
▶ **Directions:** Give each pair or group a large piece of construction paper and 1–2 paper clips. Have each pair or group make a paper airplane following a favorite design. Then have contests to see which planes can fly the farthest and the most accurately (into a wastebasket hangar) and which can do a stunt.
▶ **Variation:** Give each pair or group another sheet of paper with which to create a new sailplane design.

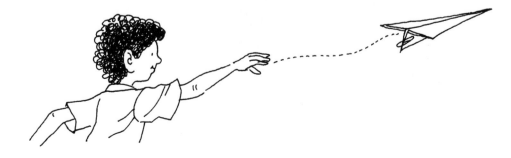

Left Hand, Right Hand

▶ **Equipment:** 2 colors of construction paper, pencils, tape

▶ **Skills:** Recognizing left and right, manual dexterity

▶ **Directions:** Have children trace their right hands on red construction paper and their left hands on lavender paper. Have them tape the papers to their appropriate hands. Players then choose to have either a right hand or a left hand hour during which the students do everything with whichever hand the class has chosen.

▶ **Hint:** Write on the chalk-board "Red-right. Lavender-left." Do not erase until the children can readily distinguish left and right.

▶ **Variations: 1.** Simon Says Left or Right: The leader does actions that involve either left or right—Simon Says wave your right hand. **2.** Shake Your Neighbor's Hand: Players tape on their red hands during work or game period. At any time, the leader can call out "Shake your neighbor's hand!" and the players shake hands with a person close by. **3.** To help players learn their right and left feet, they can trace the front of their shoes on red or lavender construction paper. Players cut out and tape the tracings to the tops of their shoes before playing Simon Says with appropriate actions—Simon says hop on your left foot. **4.** Players trace their entire left or right foot on the corresponding colors and cut it out. The leader uses the footprints to make up trails for the class to follow by stepping only with the appropriate foot on each color. **5.** Two action songs to practice right and left are the "Hokey Pokey" and "Here We Go Loop-De-Lou."

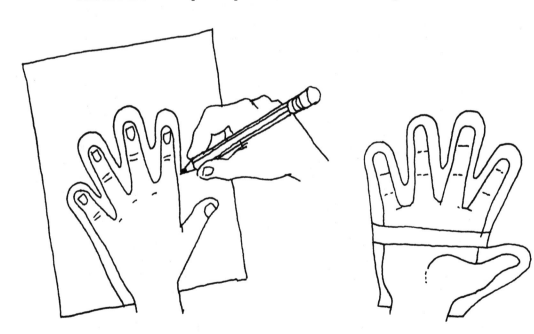

Paper Ball Team Throw

▶ **Equipment:** 1 paper ball for each player, long rope, 2 chairs
▶ **Skills:** Throwing overhand and underhand; teamwork
▶ **Setup:** 2 teams on either side of the playing area that has been divided by a rope tied to 2 chairs. To make a paper ball, wad up 1–2 sections of the Sunday newspaper (preferably the cartoon section). Secure by wrapping the ball several times with masking tape.
▶ **Directions:** At the signal, players toss the balls over the rope. Play stops after 30 seconds, and each team counts the number of balls on its side.
▶ **Scoring:** The team with the least number of paper balls scores 1 point. Play the best out of 3 rounds.
▶ **Hint:** Subtract 1 point from team's score if a player hits an opposing team member in the face or throws a ball after a signal to stop.
▶ **Variations: 1.** Have the players throw under the rope. **2.** Play Paper Ball Challenge. See Beanbag Challenge for ideas.
▶ **Adaptation:** Players in wheelchairs need another player or a way to retrieve the balls.

Paper Balls Over/Under Relay

▶ **Equipment:** 1 paper ball for each team
▶ **Skills:** Passing; teamwork; learning opposites: over/under
▶ **Setup:** Several equal teams with players lined up one behind the other
▶ **Directions:** At the signal, the first person on each team passes the ball either over his or her head or through his or her legs to the person directly behind. This person passes the ball either over or under—the opposite way it was received—to the player behind. When the ball reaches the last player, he or she runs to the head of the line and begins passing the ball again. Play continues until the first person reaches the front of the line again.
▶ **Hint:** If there are uneven numbers of players, have the first person on the team with one fewer player go twice.

Cardboard Shape Search

- **Equipment:** Several sets of cardboard shapes
- **Skills:** Teamwork; recognizing geometric shapes
- **Setup:** Divide the class into pairs, small groups, or teams. Scatter throughout the playing area several sets of cardboard shapes. Use a craft knife to cut large cardboard sheets into desired shapes.
- **Directions:** Give each group a shape or group of shapes to find. At the signal, each team finds as many of the assigned shape(s) as possible and places them in a stack. Repeat, giving each team different shapes. The teams try to improve their time with each round.
- **Variations:** 1. Cut shapes into 2–3 pieces each and have the players put together the puzzle pieces. 2. Play with cardboard numbers that teams find and place in order. 3. Write a math problem on the chalkboard and have teams search for the numbers that express the correct answer.

Cardboard Footprints

- **Equipment:** Several sets of left and right cardboard footprints
- **Skills:** Taking turns; recognizing left and right, patterns
- **Setup:** Use a craft knife to cut out left and right cardboard footprints. Scatter the footprints in different patterns throughout the playing space.
- **Directions:** Have the players step on the footprints and identify left/right and the shape or pattern of the prints. Players can take turns making up patterns for the others.
- **Hint:** Tape footprints to the playing surface if there is a danger of players slipping.

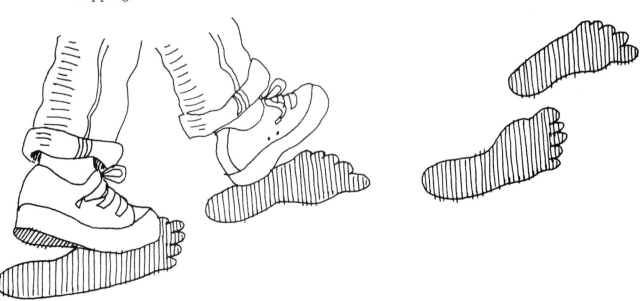

Crossover Tag

▶ **Equipment:** Cardboard shapes and numbers
▶ **Skills:** Running; recognizing shapes and numbers
▶ **Setup:** Use a craft knife to cut cardboard sheets into desired shapes and numbers. Tape them to the floor in a circle.
▶ **Directions:** Have each player stand on a cardboard shape or number. One player stands in the middle of the circle and calls out a shape or number. Players who are standing on those figures try to cross over the circle to another shape or number before the player in the middle tags them. The first person caught becomes the new tagger.
▶ **Hint:** To prevent collisions, keep the cross over groups small by using several different shapes.
▶ **Variations: 1.** Designate different locomotor movements for the players to use as they cross the circle. **2.** Have students change shapes or numbers during the game.

• •

Table-Top Shuffleboard

▶ **Equipment:** 1 cardboard game board; 8 1–inch disks, 4 of each color, for each pair of teams
▶ **Skills:** Sliding disks; partner skills
▶ **Setup:** Divide the class into teams of 2 players. Cut out and label rectangular cardboard game boards. Assemble buttons, bottle caps, checkers, etc. to use as playing disks.
▶ **Directions:** 2 teams play at a time. The first pair takes 2 turns using their fingertips to slide the disks to the other end of the game board, into the sections labeled with the highest number. Then the next pair take their turns, trying to beat the first team's score and also trying to shove the other pair's disks off the board.
▶ **Scoring:** Count each pair's total score after players have used all the disks. In order to score, more than half of a disk must land in a space.

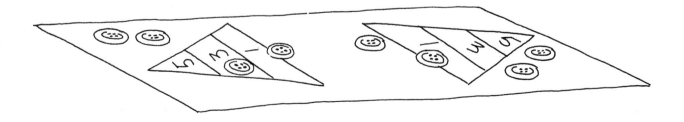

Cardboard Squares Partner Race

▶ **Equipment:** 2 pieces of cardboard each about 24 inches square for each pair of players
▶ **Skills:** Jumping; partner skills
▶ **Setup:** Partners lined up side by side on the starting line
▶ **Directions:** At the starting line, partner A holds down a piece of cardboard while partner B jumps on it. Then A places the second piece of cardboard down for B to jump on. A alternates the first and second pieces of cardboard until the partners reach the turning line. The partners return to the starting line with A jumping and B placing the cardboard squares.
▶ **Hint:** If the cardboard is too slippery, substitute foam-backed carpet squares.
▶ **Variation:** Depending on the amount of playing area and the number of players, conduct this game as a relay race with teams of partners.

Team Card Toss

▶ **Equipment:** An equal number of playing cards for each team, 1 wastebasket per team, masking tape
▶ **Skills:** Tossing; teamwork
▶ **Setup:** 2 or more teams lined up behind a masking-tape line 5–7 feet from the wastebaskets
▶ **Directions:** Each team member in turn steps up to the line and tries to toss 1 card into the wastebasket. The player then goes to the end of his or her team's line. Players continue to take turns until they have tossed all the cards. Each team counts the number of cards in its wastebasket and tries to improve its score on the next round.
▶ **Adaptations:** Players in wheelchairs can easily participate in this activity. Make sure their seatbelts are fastened and have another player hold the chair handles to prevent tipping.

Games That Use Scarves

These games and their numerous variations emphasize tossing, catching, running, and tagging skills. Children will enjoy the games that use scarves as blindfolds and the self-testing of skills in the Scarf Challenge.

Scarf Challenge

- ▶ **Equipment:** 1 scarf for each player
- ▶ **Skills:** Tossing, catching; partner skills, self-testing
- ▶ **Setup:** Players scattered throughout the playing area
- ▶ **Directions:** With each player holding a scarf, the leader challenges the players by asking the following questions:
    - •Who can make the scarf into a ball, throw it up in the air, and catch it with 2 hands? With 1 hand?
    - •Who can throw the scarf under a leg and catch it?
    - •Who can throw the scarf up and catch it on his or her head? On his or her back?
    - •Who can throw the scarf up, spin around once, and catch it?
    - •Who can show us a different trick?
    - •Which partners can toss their scarves to one another and catch them?
    - •Which partners can take turns juggling the 2 scarves?
- ▶ **Variation:** See Beanbag Challenge and Paper Tube Challenge for other ideas.

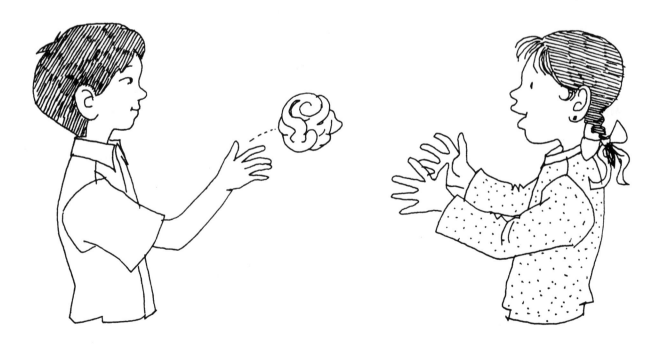

Scarf Chase

- **Equipment:** 1 scarf for each circle of players
- **Skills:** Running, tagging
- **Setup:** Players stand in a circle with their hands behind their backs
- **Directions:** The player who is It walks around the circle with a scarf. As soon as It gives the scarf to another player, It runs around the circle while the chosen player chases It and tries to tag him or her with the scarf. If It runs back to the other player's space in the circle without being tagged, the player with the scarf becomes the new It. If not, It plays another round.
- **Hints: 1.** If space permits, have several circles for more player participation. **2.** If the playing surface is slippery, change the rules to walking or skipping instead of running. **3.** To prevent collisions, have It and the player with the scarf run in opposite directions and slap right hands as they pass.
- **Variation:** Play this game with crepe paper streamers instead of scarves.

Scarf Catch

- **Equipment:** 1 scarf for each circle of players
- **Skills:** Catching
- **Setup:** Players form a circle with It in the middle
- **Directions:** It takes a large scarf, crushes it into a ball, and throws it up in the air while calling another player's name. The player called comes into the circle and tries to catch the scarf before it reaches the floor. If the scarf reaches the floor before the player catches it, she or he becomes It.
- **Hints: 1.** Make sure that It calls every player once before calling anyone a second time. **2.** If the class is large, have students form several circles.
- **Variation:** Use a beanbag instead of a scarf.

What Is This?

- ▶ **Equipment:** 1 scarf blindfold for each player
- ▶ **Skills:** Partner skills; sense perception
- ▶ **Setup:** Divide the class into partners or threes and let them pick out objects from their desks to put into small paper bags.
- ▶ **Directions:** Group members take turns wearing a scarf blindfold and trying to guess by touch what each object is in another person's bag. Repeat the game with new partners or groups.
- ▶ **Hints: 1.** Because of possible health problems such as conjunctivitis, each player should have his or her own scarf. **2.** Younger children may prefer to close their eyes tightly rather than wear a blindfold.
- ▶ **Variations: 1.** Who Said That?: Blindfold 1 player and have the other players change places in the playing area. The leader points to a player who makes a statement ("I love spring," for example) in a normal voice. The blindfolded person has 2 guesses to determine who spoke.

    2. What Is That Sound?: Have all the children wear their blindfolds while It makes a sound with something in the playing area. The first person to guess the sound correctly becomes It for the next round.
- ▶ **Hint:** Let It choose things that have been collected in a sound box (spoons, a triangle, etc.).

    3. Table Chase: 2 blindfolded players stand on either side of a long table (or 4 desks put together) with their hands on the table. Their hands must remain on the table as they move around it. Player A is the hare and player B is the hound. At the signal, the hound tries to tag the hare as both players circle the table. When the hound catches the hare, the hare becomes the hound and a new player becomes the hare.
- ▶ **Hint:** So more players can be involved, use more than 1 table or set of desks. The players who are waiting have to be as quiet as possible so the hounds and hares can hear one another. (This game can be noisy.)

    4. Animal Tag: Have several circles of players sit on chairs or on the floor. Give each seated person the name of a farm animal. The player in the middle, the "farmer" wears a blindfold. The farmer takes turns calling out the animal names, one at a time. All the players with that animal name try to exchange seats before the farmer tags them. Any player who is tagged becomes the new farmer. Whenever the farmer says, "The barn door is open!" all the players get up to change seats.
- ▶ **Hint:** Warn the children to be careful of collisions.

Games That Use Chairs

Using chairs as props is the basis for these games for individuals and teams. Teamwork, partner skills, and leadership are emphasized in games that appear in new versions of old favorites or that will be brand-new to your students.

You may want to have on hand a stopwatch or timer and a tape or cassette player or other source of music.

Numbered Chairs

▶ **Equipment:** 1 chair for each player
▶ **Skills:** Memory skills
▶ **Setup:** Players sit in chairs that are lined up, one behind the other, in 1 long line or several parallel lines
▶ **Directions:** The player in chair 1 calls out a number. The player who is sitting in that chair must immediately call out another number. If a player does not call out a number within 2–3 seconds, he or she goes to the end of the line of chairs and all players move up one chair. All the players now have a new number to remember!
▶ **Hints: 1.** Remind players to make sure they know the number of their chair before they sit down each time. **2.** For grades K–1, tape a number on the inside of each chair back.
▶ **Variations:** Identify chairs using different fruits or vegetables, letters of the alphabet, or ordinal numbers.

Move Left, Move Right!

- ▶ **Equipment:** 1 fewer chair than there are players
- ▶ **Skills:** Knowledge of left and right directions
- ▶ **Setup:** Players seated in a circle with 1 player in the middle
- ▶ **Directions:** It calls out commands for the other players to move either left or right to another seat. It starts out slowly and then speeds up. If a player moves in the wrong direction, It sits down in the empty chair, and the player without a seat becomes It.
- ▶ **Hint:** If players are not sure of left and right, have them tape on red and lavender "hands." (See Left Hand, Right Hand in the Section Games That Use Paper.)
- ▶ **Variation:** For more advanced players, It can call out simple math problems whose answers are the number of seats the players should move left or right. For example, "Left, 1+1" or "Right, 6-5".

No-Elimination Musical Chairs

- ▶ **Equipment:** 1 chair for each player
- ▶ **Skills:** Memory skills
- ▶ **Setup:** Players sit in chairs that are lined up, one behind the other, in 1 long line or several parallel lines
- ▶ **Directions:** The player in chair 1 calls out a number. The player who is sitting in that chair must immediately call out another number. If a player does not call out a number within 2–3 seconds, he or she goes to the end of the line of chairs and all players move up one chair. All the players now have a new number to remember!
- ▶ **Hints: 1.** Remind players to make sure they know the number of their chair before they sit down each time. **2.** For grades K–1, tape a number on the inside of each chair back.
- ▶ **Variations:** Identify chairs using different fruits or vegetables, letters of the alphabet, or ordinal numbers.

Team Chair Relay

▶ **Equipment:** 1 chair for each player
▶ **Skills:** Walking, running; teamwork
▶ **Setup:** 2 teams, with each team sitting in a circle of chairs facing out from the center
▶ **Directions:** At the signal, 1 member of each team gets up and runs once around the circle and back to his or her chair. The player sits down and slaps the hand of the player to the left. Play continues until everyone has had a turn. Teams try to improve their race times in each round.
▶ **Variations: 1.** Have players move their chairs far enough apart so that players can weave in and out around the circle. **2.** Change the formation to lines rather than circles of chairs and continue play.

Chair Simon Says

▶ **Equipment:** 1 chair for each player
▶ **Skills:** Following directions, imitating actions
▶ **Setup:** Players seated on their chairs scattered throughout the playing area with the leader seated in front of the group
▶ **Directions:** The leader calls out movements that players can do while seated. The first player who is caught not following the command correctly becomes the new leader.
▶ **Variation:** Up! Down!: The leader and the other players start the game by standing in front of their chairs. The leader gives a command that means the opposite—"Stand up!" means the players should sit down, and vice versa. The first player who sits instead of stands or vice versa becomes the new leader.
▶ **Hint: 1.** For younger children, have the leader sit or stand even though he or she says the opposite. **2.** Change leaders after every 5 commands.

Chair Volleyball

▶ **Equipment:** Chairs facing in alternating directions to divide the playing area, large beach ball or balloon

▶ **Skills:** Tapping a ball with 1 or 2 hands; teamwork

▶ **Setup:** 2 teams, on either side of the playing area

▶ **Directions:** Have the teams volley for serve. Play continues until the ball goes out of bounds—touching the ceiling or floor. Players can hit the ball as many times as they want. They can also catch the ball and throw it again. Players can serve the ball from anywhere they want.

▶ **Scoring:** 1 point for each out-of-bounds ball for the other team. 9 points wins. Play the best out of 3 or 5 games.

▶ **Hints: 1.** Each player should have a turn to serve before anyone gets a second turn. **2.** Do not allow "spiking." **3.** If the playing area is wide enough, set up 2 separate courts for 4 teams.

▶ **Variations: 1.** To give more players an opportunity to play, rotate teams of 5 players after every point or after 1 minute. **2.** Play the game using 6 beach balls. The team with the least number of balls on its side receives 1 point. Play several rounds. **3.** Play according to the original rules. In addition, any time the leader blows a whistle, the person holding or hitting the ball has to do a penalty such as singing a song or reciting a poem or nursery rhyme. **4.** Use a length of clothesline or rope instead of chains to divide the playing area.

Over-the-Chair Bounce

▶ **Equipment:** 1 chair, 1 ball, and 1 cardboard box or wastebasket for each team
▶ **Skills:** Bouncing; teamwork
▶ **Setup:** 2 or more teams lined up behind a masking-tape line about 6 feet away from a chair. On the other side of the chair place a wastebasket or box.
▶ **Directions:** At the signal, the first player on each team tries to bounce the ball over the chair and into the basket. Play continues until everyone has had a turn.
▶ **Scoring:** 1 point for each basket. Teams keep track of their scores, totaling them after each team member has taken a turn. Play again, with each team trying to improve in previous score.

Chair Challenge

▶ **Equipment:** 1 chair for each player
▶ **Skills:** Varied locomotor movements; self-testing; creative thinking
▶ **Setup:** Players and chairs in lines or circles
▶ **Directions:** The leader challenges the players by asking the following questions:
 •Who can sit up straight on his or her chair?
 •Who can walk around the chair slowly? Quickly?
 •Who can skip around the chair?
 •Who can move around the chair in a different way?
 •Who can raise his or her right hand and run around the chair to the right? To the left?
 •Who can think of something new to do with the chair?
 •Who can find a partner and think of something new to do with the chairs?

Chair Exercise Challenge

▶ **Equipment:** 1 chair for each player

▶ **Skills:** Strengthening; self-testing; partner and leadership skills

▶ **Setup:** Players seated on their chairs in rows, with 1 leader-demonstrator in front of the group

▶ **Directions:** The leader challenges the players by asking the following questions:

•While a partner holds the back of the chair steady, who can step up and down on the chair 10 times alternating feet? 10 times leading with the right foot? 10 times leading with the left foot?

•Who can do 10 pushups? (Players face their chairs with their hands on either side of the chair seat. Who can do 10 tricep pushups? (Players stand with their backs to the chair and their hands on either side of the seat.)

•Who can lift his or her feet, one at a time, and then straighten the leg to point straight ahead, 10 times each leg? (Players hold the chair seat with both hands.)

•Who can lift both legs at the same time and flutter-kick for 30 seconds? (Players hold the chair seat with both hands.)

•Who can link hands behind his or her head and twist slowly back and forth?

•Who can stand behind the chair and lift it up to chest height 10 times? (Players bend their knees as they lift.)

•Who can make up a different exercise using a chair?

▶ **Hints: 1.** Encourage children to breathe normally during the exercises and to keep their backs straight and their abdomens held in tightly. **2.** Start with 1 set of each exercise and increase to 2–3 sets each exercise period. Work up to at least 3 days a week, alternating with cardiovascular exercises such as jogging, dancing, or rope jumping. **3.** You may want to have the children do these exercises during the last 15 minutes before class or at the end of the day. Players can keep their own fitness charts. **4.** If necessary, get parental and medical permission before starting this or any other exercise program.

Games That Use Clothesline

Several of these games are meant as alternate activities for rhythmic rope jumping, which can be very frustrating for children in the lower grades. While having fun with these games and activities, players will gain the necessary confidence in using ropes to enable them to master future rope jumping skills.

For all these games, tape the ends of the clothesline or rope with plastic tape to keep them from fraying. Have players observe this basic safety rule: They should never put a rope around their neck or anyone else's.

Jump the Magic Rope

▶ **Equipment:** 1 clothesline
▶ **Skills:** Jumping, leaping; taking turns
▶ **Setup:** Players standing in line. Tie one end of the clothesline to a chair and give the other end to a player.
▶ **Directions:** The player holding the rope shakes it back and forth in small "S" shapes as players try not to step on the squiggles. Players in turn leap or jump over the magic rope.
▶ **Hints: 1.** Before playing this game, have children practice jumping on 2 feet, using their arms to help them go upward and landing on the balls of their feet with their knees slightly bent. To practice, you may want to play Jump the Candles in the section Games That Use Paper or Jump the Alligator in the section Games That Use Beanbags. **2.** Use several clotheslines so there is less waiting. **3.** To prevent collisions, players wait on the other side after their turn. **4.** Instruct any player holding a rope to hold it loosely and to let go immediately if someone's foot becomes caught on it.
▶ **Variations: 1.** Earth Tremors: The player holding the rope shakes it up and down, making small bumps that players try not to step on. **2.** Over the Swinging Rope: The player holding the rope swings it gently from side to side as players try to leap over it. **3.** Have several players stand in a line parallel to one side of a long rope. At the signal, have the players jump back and forth over the rope, beginning with 1 jump on either side and then trying a double jump. You can teach this popular rope jumping skill by having the players chant "Big, little, big, little," and jumping higher on "big" and lower on "little." Players may want to jump to rope jumping rhymes they know.

Rope Circle

▶ **Equipment:** 1 length of clothesline tied in a circle large enough to accommodate all the players
▶ **Skills:** Balancing, walking, jumping, hopping; group work
▶ **Setup:** Tie the ends of a length of clothesline together and have players stand in a circle and grasp it with both hands.
▶ **Directions:** Have all the players do the following activities together.
- •Touch your head, chest, waist, knees, and toes with the rope.
- •On a count of 3, toss the rope up and catch it.
- •Pass the rope to the right/left. Walk and turn while switching hands.
- •Place the rope on the floor and walk to the left/right on it, balancing with each foot.
- •Jump/hop/step from side to side over the rope.
- •Do 5/10 sit-ups, touching the rope to your bent knees.
- •Lie on your stomach, look under the rope, and wave good-bye.

Who Has the Ring?

▶ **Equipment:** Clothesline with a curtain ring threaded onto it
▶ **Skills:** Guessing; passing
▶ **Setup:** Slide a curtain ring onto a length of clothesline and knot the ends. Have the players sit in a circle holding the rope with both hands.
▶ **Directions:** Pick a player to be It who stands in the middle of the circle and closes his or her eyes. At the signal, players begin passing the ring around the rope. When It calls "stop" the player nearest the ring covers it with one hand. It has 2 guesses to name who has the ring. If he or she cannot guess, the person covering the ring becomes It.
▶ **Variation:** Add additional curtain rings until there is 1 fewer the number of seated players. It then has to guess who does not have the ring.

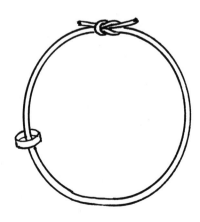

Clothesline Quoits

▶ **Equipment:** 4 rope rings for every 2 players, plastic bottle target pins
▶ **Skills:** Tossing for accuracy; partner skills
▶ **Setup:** Divide the class into pairs. Set up target pins (have some players take test throws to see what is a challenging but fair distance for that grade level). To make rope rings, see directions in Part Three, Making and Adapting Equipment.
▶ **Directions:** Players each throw 2 rings at the pins.
▶ **Scoring:** 5 points for a ringer and 1 point if the rope ring hits the target pin. Pairs try to improve their score with each round.

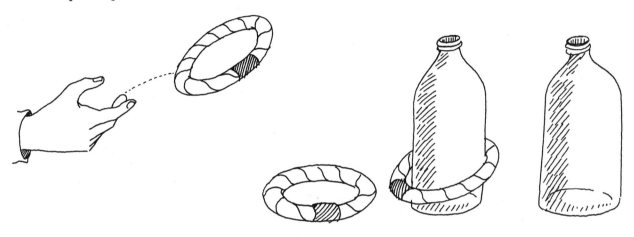

Short Rope Challenge

▶ **Equipment:** 1 7–8 foot length of clothesline for each player
▶ **Skills:** Jumping, hopping, skipping, galloping; creative thinking; partner skills
▶ **Setup:** Players scattered throughout the playing area
▶ **Directions:** Hand out the ropes and challenge the players to do the following actions with them:
  •Who can balance on the rope walking forwards? Backwards?
  •Who can leap over the rope?
  •Who can jump over the rope? Turn in the air while jumping?
  •Who can straddle the ropes and walk with 1 foot on either side?
  •Who can skip around the rope? Gallop around it?
  •Who can go over the rope a different way?
  •Who can make a square with the rope? What can you pretend it is—a TV, a cube, a box?
  •Who can make a triangle with the rope? What is it—a chocolate kiss, a tower, a spaceship?
  •Who can make his or her own shape—a surfboard, a race track, a pretzel?
  •Who can make a bigger and different shape with someone else?

Games That Use Masking Tape

In addition to these games, you can use masking tape for start and finish lines, foul lines, and game boundary lines. You can also use it to make shapes, footprints, or other patterns for the players to follow. Masking-tape lines can define squares for tossing games or mark individual spaces on the floor to help players organize the full amount of playing area. Remember to pull up masking tape promptly, before it becomes difficult to remove. Masking tape is also helpful in making paper balls, flying disks, and other equipment.

Stoplight

▶ **Equipment:** Masking tape, 1 cardboard box for each player, 1 sheet red construction paper labeled *Stop!*, 1 sheet green construction paper labeled *Go!*

▶ **Skills:** Pushing; group work

▶ **Setup:** Put down a large circle of masking tape on the playing surface.

▶ **Directions:** Players place their cardboard "cars" on the tape, grasp the sides with either hand, and begin pushing their cars in the same direction around the "road." The leader or "traffic officer" stands in the middle of the circle with the 2 sheets of construction paper that he or she holds up as commands to the drivers to stop and go. Players follow the commands of the officer without crashing into another car or driver. Any driver who does not obey the officer gets a ticket, a slip of yellow paper on which is written a penalty. Encourage players to listen to and follow the officer's commands without getting any tickets. Change leaders after several commands.

▶ **Variation:** Make a drivers' obstacle course around the entire playing area. The masking-tape road should weave around obstacles such as boxes, ropes, and milk cartons. Players try to complete the course without knocking down anything near the road.

Team Balance Beam

▶ **Equipment:** 1 long strip of masking tape for each team, balls
▶ **Skills:** Tossing, catching; teamwork
▶ **Setup:** Place the 2 masking-tape "balance beams" on the floor and have the 2 teams line up facing each other.
▶ **Directions:** Teams try to toss and catch balls without stepping off the beams.
▶ **Scoring:** A player who does step off the beam earns the team 1 penalty point. At the end of play, the team with the most points has to sing a song that the other team chooses.

High Wire Challenge

▶ **Equipment:** 1 line of masking tape 4–5 feet long for each player
▶ **Skills:** Balancing; partner skills; creative thinking
▶ **Setup:** Players scattered throughout the playing area
▶ **Directions:** Have each player place a strip of masking tape on the playing surface. Tell the players to imagine the tape is a circus high wire. Challenge them to do the following activities without falling off:
•Who can walk forwards (heel to toe) on the tape without falling off? Backwards? Sideways?
•Who can jump up and land on the tape without losing his or her balance?
•Who can walk, turn on his or her toes, and walk in the other direction without falling off?
•Who can walk on the tape while balancing a beanbag on his or her head?
•Who can leap over a beanbag that is on the tape? Toss it up and catch it? Hop over it with one foot?
•Who can keep hitting a balloon up in the air without stepping off the tape?
•Who can balance on 1 hand and foot on the tape?
•Who can "monkey scamper" (move on all fours) along the tape?
•Who can make up a balancing trick?
•Who can make up a balancing trick with 1–2 other players?

Games That Use Tin Cans

To prepare for these games, remove the lids from juice, tuna fish, fruit, or soup cans. Wash the cans and sand the inside edges. You may want to alert parents to save cans for your class.

In addition to stacking and balancing skills, these games also encourage creative thinking, imitation of locomotor movements and rhythms, and teamwork.

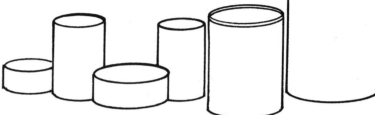

Miniature Golf

- ▶ **Equipment:** Large juice or soup cans, yardsticks, floor hockey sticks, or long cardboard tubes, indoor golf balls or wiffleballs, beanbags or boxes
- ▶ **Skills:** Putting; partner skills
- ▶ **Setup:** With the class, set up a 9– or 18–hole golf course. Sink tin cans into the ground or turn them on their sides. Scatter beanbags or boxes as obstacles for players to putt around. Divide the class into pairs.
- ▶ **Directions:** Pairs take turns trying to putt the golf ball into each hole with the fewest number of strokes or hits. Players total their number of strokes at the completion of the course. On the next round, have players try to improve their score by using fewer strokes.
- ▶ **Variation:** Use brooms to sweep rather than putt the ball.
- ▶ **Adaptations:** For children in wheelchairs, set up the course on a smooth playing surface such as blacktop, cement, or tile, and make a golf club from a broomstick or hockey stick.

Tuna-Can Stilts

▶ **Equipment:** 2 tuna fish or similar cans per player, strong twine or rope
▶ **Skills:** Balancing
▶ **Setup:** Poke 2 holes in the top of each can and thread strong twine through the holes. Bring the ends of the twine up to the waist height of each player and knot the ends.
▶ **Directions:** Players put 1 foot on the top of each can and hold onto the knotted ropes. Players try to walk around without losing their balance.
▶ **Hint:** This game is best to play on a carpeted or dry grassy area to prevent damage to the floor or soft earth and to cushion any falls.
▶ **Variation:** Have players use their stilts to walk on a masking-tape balance beam or high wire.

• •

Tin-Can Towers

▶ **Equipment:** Enough cans of varied sizes to make a pile
▶ **Skills:** Balancing; teamwork
▶ **Setup:** 3–4 small teams standing behind a line
▶ **Directions:** At the signal, the first player from each team runs to the pile of cans, grabs 1, and takes it back to his or her teammates, who begin to make tin-can towers. The second players then race to the pile of cans, and so on. Teams try to see how high they can stack the cans before their tower falls. Have each team try again, and then form new teams to try one more time.
▶ **Variation:** Use a selection of small boxes instead of tin cans for stacking.

Games That Use Brooms

Children use whiskbrooms, push brooms, and regular brooms to play floor hockey, table-top hockey, and shuffleboard, as well as other games that involve teamwork or partner skills. Sweeping, passing, and catching are among the important motor skills.

Broom Hockey

▶ **Equipment:** 1 regular broom for each player, goal markers or large box for goal, 4–inch playground or yarn balls, chair

▶ **Skills:** Sweeping, passing; teamwork

▶ **Setup:** Divide the class into 2 teams and then into squads of 3–5 players, with 1 player in each squad as goalie

▶ **Directions:** Start the game in the center of the playing area with a signal from the referee. At the same time, the referee drops the ball between 2 players. Players try to make a goal by sweeping the ball between the goal markers. Any player who takes the broom off the floor or purposely runs into another player sits in a "penalty box" (chair) for 1 minute. Goalies can use their hands and feet to stop the balls, and no player can challenge the goalie when he or she has touched a ball. Change squads every 3 minutes.

▶ **Hints: 1.** Cut broom handles down (and tape the ends) to fit the average size of the players. **2.** This game works best with grades 2 and up. **3.** If your playing area is small, allow teams of only 3 players.

▶ **Variations: 1.** Add 1 or more balls and allow 2 goalies per team. **2.** Use balls of different sizes.

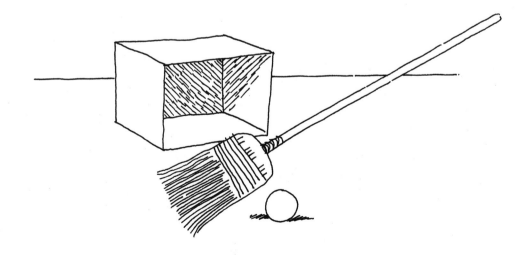

Team Sweep

▶ **Equipment:** 1 paper ball and 1 broom for each player, masking tape
▶ **Skills:** Sweeping; teamwork
▶ **Setup:** 2 teams on either side of the playing area that has been divided by a line of masking tape
▶ **Directions:** At the signal, players sweep the balls across the dividing line. Play stops after 30 seconds, and each team counts the number of balls on its side.
▶ **Scoring:** The team with the fewest balls on its side scores 1 point. Play the best out of 3 rounds.

Push-Broom Shuffleboard

▶ **Equipment:** 2 push brooms; 8 plastic floor hockey pucks, 4 of each color; masking tape
▶ **Skills:** Sliding disks; partner skills
▶ **Setup:** Divide the class into teams of 2 players. Mark the foul and scoring lines with masking tape.
▶ **Directions:** 2 teams play at a time. The first pair takes 2 turns to use the broom to push the puck to the other end of the playing area, into the section labeled with the highest number. Then the next pair take their turns, trying to beat the first team's score and also trying to knock the other pair's puck off the playing area.
▶ **Scoring:** Count each pair's total score after players have used all the pucks. In order to score, more than half of a puck must land in a space.
▶ **Hint:** Make sure the playing surface is smooth and clean.

Whiskbroom Table Hockey

▶ **Equipment:** 1 whiskbroom per player, long tables, table tennis balls
▶ **Skills:** Teamwork
▶ **Setup:** Divide the class into 2 teams. Sit an equal number of players from each team around a long table.
▶ **Directions:** The leader drops the ball onto the middle of the table, and players try to sweep the ball into their designated goals at the end of the table. Players who are sitting at the ends are the goalies, who can stop the balls with their hands. Each time a team scores a goal, have all players shift 1 seat to the left so that teams and goalies are constantly changing. If a ball bounces over a player, he or she takes a free sweep.
▶ **Hint:** Encourage players to keep their brooms on the table at all times and to sweep with only 1 hand.
▶ **Variations: 1.** Use several balls at the same time, a different color for each team. **2.** Use plastic spoons or unsharpened pencils with large erasers on the end instead of whiskbrooms.

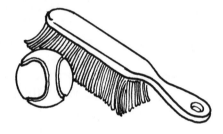

Catch the Broomstick

▶ **Equipment:** 1 broom for each circle
▶ **Skills:** Catching
▶ **Setup:** Divide the class into as many groups as there are brooms available. Have the players form a circle (with their backs to the center) around a chosen player who is holding a broom upright.
▶ **Directions:** The player in the center calls out a name and at the same time lets go of the broom. The player who was called turns around and quickly runs to the center to catch the broom before it touches the playing surface. If the player catches it in time, he or she goes to the center. If the player misses, the player in the center calls out another name.

Games That Use Sheets

A guessing game, a team ball game, and a variation on Simon Says are among the activities in this section. They emphasize following directions, creative thinking, and locomotor movements. Most of the games require no materials other than a large sheet.

Team Shake

▶ **Equipment:** 1 large sheet for each group, yarn balls
▶ **Skills:** Teamwork
▶ **Setup:** Divide the class into as many groups as there are sheets available. Players stand around the sheet, holding it with both hands. The leader designates 2 teams by dividing the number of players holding each half of the sheet. Put at least 12 yarn balls in the center of each sheet.
▶ **Directions:** At the signal, each team tries to shake the balls out of the sheet and over the heads of the opposing team. Players can hit the balls back into the center of the sheet with 1 hand. When all the balls have been shaken out, the leader counts the balls on the playing surface behind each team. Replace the balls in the center of the sheet and play again. Each team tries to improve its score.
▶ **Variation:** Use balls of a different color for each team and see which team can shake out all its balls first.
▶ **Adaptation:** If some children are in wheelchairs, have players sit on chairs so that everyone is at the same level.

Who's Under the Sheet?

▶ **Equipment:** 1 large sheet
▶ **Skills:** Guessing
▶ **Setup:** Designate 1–2 players as guessers who turn their back to the group. The rest of the players sit with the sheet draped over them.
▶ **Directions:** At the signal, the guessers turn around and tap a player who is seated under the sheet. The guessers ask, "Who is this under the sheet?" The tapped player says, "I am under the sheet." The guessers have 2 tries to identify the players from the sound of their voices. If they guess correctly, the identified players become the guessers for the next round.
▶ **Hints: 1.** Players may not disguise their voices. **2.** If your group is large, use more than 1 sheet.

Carousel

▶ **Equipment:** 1 large sheet for each group
▶ **Skills:** Locomotor movements; group work; following directions
▶ **Setup:** Divide the class into groups. Players in each group use 1 hand to hold a sheet at waist level.
▶ **Directions:** The leader calls out a locomotor movement for all players to do in the same direction. On a whistle signal, the leader calls out, "Reverse!" and the players do the same movement in the other direction. Change leaders after several calls.
▶ **Hints: 1.** Add music to encourage rhythmic movements. **2.** Have a stop signal in case any player trips or falls. **3.** Players should hold the sheet with both hands if they are sliding.

Birthday Exchange

- **Equipment:** 2 or more large sheets sewn together
- **Skills:** Group work; recognizing birth dates
- **Setup:** Players hold the sheets with both hands on the playing surface
- **Directions:** On the count of 3, players slowly raise the sheet as high as they can. As they do this, the leader calls out 3–4 months of the year. If players have a birthday in one of those months, they cross under the sheets to find a new place on the other side. Players holding the sheets try to lower them to the ground before the birthday players find a new place.
- **Hint:** To prevent collisions, have players put 1 hand in front of their faces as they scramble for new places.

. . . .

Flying Saucer

- **Equipment:** 1 large sheet
- **Skills:** Group work; following directions
- **Setup:** Players in a squatting position hold the sheet with both hands
- **Directions:** On the count of 3, players raise the sheet as high as they can. Then the leader signals for everyone to let go and stand still as the sheet becomes a flying saucer and floats to the floor on the players' heads. Players do not move until the sheet has landed on the floor.

. . . .

Sheet Stunt

- **Equipment:** 1 large sheet
- **Skills:** Creative thinking; group work
- **Setup:** Players holding a sheet with both hands
- **Directions:** Give each player a number. When the leader calls their number, players go under the sheet that the other players lift up and then drop. The players under the sheet work together to create a stunt or exercise that they perform when the sheet is lifted again. Continue until all the players have had a turn to plan a stunt.

Games That Use Tires and Hoops

Bicycle tires, car tires, and plastic hoops are the basic equipment for these games. Teams and partners will enjoy practicing jumping, balancing, and other locomotor skills.

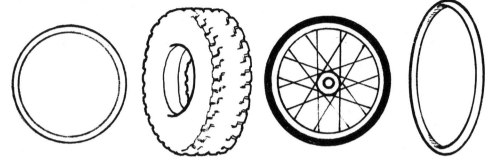

Tire Roll

▶ **Equipment:** 1 car tire for each group
▶ **Skills:** Rolling; taking turns
▶ **Setup:** Groups of pairs or threes
▶ **Directions:** Players take turns rolling a car tire to one another. They try to roll it hard enough so that it reaches the other player before it falls over. Players see how far apart they can stand and still roll the tire to the other players.
▶ **Hint:** This is a good activity to increase arm and upper body strength.

Tire Balance

▶ **Equipment:** 1 car tire for each pair
▶ **Skills:** Balancing; partner skills
▶ **Setup:** Place tires flat throughout the playing area.
▶ **Directions:** To begin, players put a hand on their partner's shoulder as the partner walks around the tire with them. Players then try to walk around on the tires alone without falling off. Players see whether they can balance more easily with arms extended, up in the air, and so on.
▶ **Variation:** Players try to challenge their partners by asking if they can stand on 1 foot, jump on the tire with both feet, and so forth.

Tire Tunes

▶ **Equipment:** Bicycle tires or inner tubes, music
▶ **Skills:** Balancing, agility
▶ **Setup:** Place a number of tires throughout the playing area.
▶ **Directions:** Players in turn follow a path of tires across the playing area, trying to step in and out of the tires in time to the music. Vary the tempo of the music to keep the game exciting, and have players change the layout of the tires.
▶ **Hints: 1.** This game helps players improve their footwork. **2.** To cut down on waiting time, set up several playing areas.

Partner Tire Race

▶ **Equipment:** 2 26-inch bicycle tires for each pair of players, or inner tubes
▶ **Skills:** Jumping; partner skills
▶ **Setup:** Partners lined up side by side on the starting line
▶ **Directions:** At the starting line, partner A holds a tire down while partner B jumps into it. Then A places the second tire down for B to jump into. A alternates the first and second tires until the partners reach the turning line. The partners return to the starting line with A jumping and B holding the tires.
▶ **Variations: 1.** Use only 1 tire and have partners alternate jumping and holding. **2.** Players take turns either stepping into the tire and bringing it up over their head or holding the tire up over their head and then bringing it down and stepping through it. **3.** Conduct this game as a relay race with teams of partners.

Hoop Shoot

▶ **Equipment:** 2 large plastic hoops, 2 large beach balls
▶ **Skills:** Throwing; taking turns
▶ **Setup:** Tie the hoops to the backs of standard basketball hoops. Divide the class in half, with 1 group playing at each basket.
▶ **Directions:** Players take turns shooting balls through the hoops. Each player has 3 tries. Players try to improve their score on each round.
▶ **Hint:** This game is very successful with younger children who like to shoot baskets but usually do not have the strength to throw balls up and through standard basketball hoops.
▶ **Variations: 1.** Players throw a football through the hoop. **2.** To make the game more difficult, have the hoop spin while players attempt to throw the football through it.

Hoop Challenge

▶ **Equipment:** 1 large plastic hoop for each player
▶ **Skills:** Locomotor movements; partner skills; creative thinking
▶ **Setup:** Players scattered throughout the playing area with enough room to move with their hoops
▶ **Directions:** The leader challenges players by asking the following questions:
  • Who can jump in and out of the hoop? Hop in and out?
  • Who can move the hoop around his or her waist? Knees? Another part of the body?
  • Who can roll the hoop and run beside it? Gallop beside it?
  • Who can spin the hoop on the floor?
  • Who can make up a trick with the hoop?
  • Which partners can roll their hoops to each other at the same time and catch them before they fall over?
  • Which partners can spin 2 hoops on their body at the same time?
  • Who can roll 1 hoop while his or her partner goes through it?
  • Which partner can make up a new trick using both hoops?
▶ **Variation:** See Rope Challenge for other ideas.

Games That Use Balls and Balloons

Beach balls, yarn balls, table tennis balls, and balloons are all part of the fun of these games. For directions on making yarn or sock balls or taping Velcro to table tennis balls, see Part Three, Making and Adapting Equipment.
You may want to look at the section Games That Use Beanbags. You can often substitute different kinds and sizes of balls for the beanbags in those games.
For safety, teachers should blow up the balloons and discourage players from putting them in their mouth.

Beach Ball Tap

▶ **Equipment:** 1 large beach ball for each circle of players
▶ **Skills:** Jumping, tapping, passing; partner skills
▶ **Setup:** 2 teams, each forming a circle
▶ **Directions:** Each team picks 2 players to stand in the center of the other team's circle. At the signal, each circle of players tries to pass the beach ball back and forth over the heads of the players in the center. The 2 players in the center try to hit the beach ball out of the circle to score a point for their team.

Beach Ball Pass, Roll, and Dodge

▶ **Equipment:** 1–3 large beach balls
▶ **Skills:** Passing, rolling, dodging; teamwork
▶ **Setup:** Players in a large circle with 3–4 players in the center
▶ **Directions:** Players in the circle hold the beach balls. At the signal, players roll the beach balls into the center, trying to hit the feet of the players who are trying to dodge the balls. If a beach ball misses a player and rolls to other side, the player who picks up the ball passes it to another player who then rolls it back into the center. If a ball hits a player in the center, he or she changes places with the player in the circle who rolled the ball.
▶ **Hints: 1.** Passing the beach ball ensures that everyone has a chance to roll the ball. **2.** If there is room, have several playing circles so there is more action.

Circle Pattern Toss

▶ **Equipment:** 1 yarn or sock ball for each circle of players
▶ **Skills:** Tossing, catching, memory skills
▶ **Setup:** Divide the class into small circles, each with 1 yarn or sock ball.
▶ **Directions:** At the signal, the player holding the ball tosses it to another player. The player who receives the ball tosses it to another player and so on until everyone has had a turn to receive and toss the ball. Then players try to repeat the pattern by tossing the ball to the person they tossed it to before. If a player drops the ball or tosses it to the wrong person, he or she moves to another circle.
▶ **Hint:** For younger children, keep the circles small and use larger balls if players have trouble catching the yarn or sock balls.
▶ **Variations: 1.** For grades 2–3, have a leader call out "Reverse!" at random, thereby challenging players to reverse the tossing pattern—tossing the ball back to the player who threw it to them. **2.** Use 2 balls for more action but have players continue to follow the pattern of the first ball.

• •

Egg Carton Bounce

▶ **Equipment:** 6 table tennis or small rubber balls for each group, 1 egg carton or cupcake pan for each group
▶ **Skills:** Bouncing; partner skills
▶ **Setup:** Divide the class into twos or threes and give each group 6 balls and an egg carton or cupcake pan.
▶ **Directions:** Players stand behind a line and take turns trying to bounce balls into the compartments. Players try to improve their score with each turn. Have groups see how far away from the egg cartons they can stand and still bounce the balls into the compartments.
▶ **Variation:** Substitute large buttons for the balls and have players pitch them directly into the compartments.

Table Tennis Targets

▶ **Equipment:** Table tennis balls with strips of Velcro glued to them, felt or flannel target (see Making and Adapting Equipment in Part Three)
▶ **Skills:** Throwing (overhand), tossing (underhand); teamwork
▶ **Setup:** Teams of 3–4 players
▶ **Directions:** Players take turns tossing or throwing table tennis balls at the target. Each player has 1–3 tries.
▶ **Scoring:** 1 point for each ball that hits the target.
▶ **Variations: 1.** Play Tick, Tack, Toe, tossing or throwing 3 balls at the target in a line or on a diagonal. **2.** See how far away players can stand and still hit the target. **3.** Use a target board on which you have written random numbers. Players try to throw or toss the balls to gain the highest score possible.
▶ **Hints:** Younger children find it easier to toss rather than throw the balls. Allow them to stand closer to the target.
▶ **Adaptations:** Children in wheelchairs need another child to help them or a way to retrieve balls. They may also need to move closer to the target.

Balloon Basketball

▶ **Equipment:** 2 large cardboard carton "baskets," 4 large balloons, 2 of each color
▶ **Skills:** Tapping, catching, passing; teamwork
▶ **Setup:** Divide the class into 2 teams, half of each team scattered on either side of the playing area. Place a basket at each end of the playing area.
▶ **Directions:** Play starts at the center line as each team taps and passes its 2 balloons among each of its players. After each player has had a turn, team members can try to tap the balloons into their basket. No player can be closer than 3 feet from a basket, and no player who is holding a balloon can move his or her feet. Players from the opposing team try to prevent baskets by catching the balloons.
▶ **Scoring:** The first team to get both balloons into its basket gets 1 point. The first quarter ends, and play starts again from the center. If any player touches another player, it counts as a foul. The fouled player gets a free tap to the team's basket from where he or she is standing.
▶ **Variation:** Use unsharpened pencils to tap the balloons.

Team Balloon Hit-Over

▶ **Equipment:** 1 large balloon for each player
▶ **Skills:** Hitting, tapping; teamwork
▶ **Setup:** Divide the class into 2 teams seated in 2 facing lines of chairs arranged 1 foot apart. Each player has a balloon on his or her lap.
▶ **Directions:** At the signal, players try to hit their balloons over the heads of the opposing team while trying to stop the other team's balloons from going over their heads. Teams hit the balloons back and forth for 3 minutes. The leader then counts the balloons that have landed on the floor behind each team. Play 2 more rounds so each team can try to better its score. Then mix and change teams and repeat 2–3 times.

Balloon-in-the-Air

▶ **Equipment:** 1 large balloon for each 2–3 players
▶ **Skills:** Tapping; partner skills
▶ **Setup:** Groups of 2–3 players, each with 1 large balloon
▶ **Directions:** At the signal, players see how long they can keep a balloon in the air by taking turns hitting it.
▶ **Hint:** Larger balloons are easier for younger players to hit.
▶ **Variations: 1.** Have players try to hit the balloon 100 times. **2.** Players hit the balloon with 1 hand only. **3.** Give each player a balloon for an individual activity. **4.** Set up an obstacle course for players to walk around while keeping their balloons up in the air. Have players sit in a chair; weave around milk cartons, hit through a hoop, etc.
▶ **Adaptations:** If some players are in wheelchairs, have the rest of the players sit in chairs. You may want to eliminate or adapt the obstacle course.

PART TWO

Activities for
Special Occasions

Activities for Special Occasions

You may want to use these activities that combine stunts and skills to celebrate special days in your class or school. All the games and activities emphasize participation, not keeping score. The section begins appropriately with warm-ups and fitness and strength exercises for any occasion.

All-Occasion Warm-ups

Stretches or slow movement exercises are good warm-ups before strenuous games. Warm-ups that are slow, rhythmic, and controlled help pulled or torn muscles and ligaments. They also help children get ready mentally for game situations. In addition to the warm-ups given here, tag games, obstacle courses, relays, and activity circuits (all in this section) are also appropriate.

1. **MUSICAL WHISTLE WARM-UPS:** Have players scatter around the playing space. The leader starts by playing slow then faster music. The players stay in position and do their own exercises to the rhythm of the music. Whenever the leader blows a whistle, (approximately every 15–20 seconds) players start doing a different exercise of their choice. The entire warm-up period can be 2–5 minutes.

2. **MUSICAL RUN:** Set up 4 markers in various parts of the playing area. Attach to each marker a slip of paper with the name of the movement players do while they move to the next marker. Movements include slow jogging, hopping, leaping over tape strips, and skipping. This warm-up is more fun to the rhythm of popular music.

▶ **Hint:** Encourage the children to move in single file and not to pass one another.

▶ **Adaptation:** Differently abled students can use the center of the playing area. If there are movements they can not do, have them choose.

3. **MUSICAL IMAGINATIVE MOVEMENTS:** Players scatter around the playing area. Play different kinds of mood music that children might associate with feelings of happiness, anger, sadness, and so on, and have players move in a way that fits the mood.

Exercises for Fitness and Strength

Players can do these exercises before class starts in the morning or at recess. You may want to have children do fitness exercises 3 times a week and alternate with strength exercises. As always, music makes these exercises more fun.

Start slowly with 5–10 repetitions of each exercise and build up over time to 25 repetitions. Make sure players wear non-slippery, comfortable shoes.

1. **SIDE-TO-SIDE JUMP:** Players put their feet and legs together and jump on both feet from side to side over a tape strip or an imaginary line.
2. **IMAGINARY ROPE JUMPING:** Players pretend they are turning a jump rope and jump with 1 or 2 feet over the imaginary rope.
3. **WOOD CHOPPER:** Players stand in a straddle position with both their hands clasped together over their heads. With their knees slightly bent, they bring their hands down between their feet as though they are chopping wood.
4. **FRONT-TO-BACK JUMP:** Players put their feet and legs together and take small jumps forward and backward.
5. **HAND-WALKER:** With their feet together, players bend down and touch the floor with both hands. They "walk" forward on their hands until they are almost completely prone and then "walk" back toward their feet.
6. **WEATHERVANE:** Players stand with their feet a shoulder-width apart and their hands locked behind their heads. They slowly rotate their elbows and upper body as if being blown by the wind.
7. **JOGGING IN PLACE:** Players move their arms and feet as though they are jogging but stay in one spot.
8. **DANCING:** Players dance in place, using any creative movements they want.

5.

Strength Exercises

Players should breath normally while doing these exercises and not hold their breath. Players should not arch their backs during these exercises. You may want to provide carpet squares as little exercise mats.

1. **JET PLANE:** Players stand in one place and extend their arms at shoulder level to imitate a plane flying for up to 20 seconds.
2. **V-SIT:** Players while extending their legs and arms in a V try to keep their balance for up to 20 seconds.
   ▶ **Hint:** Have players sit on a carpet square or other soft surface.
3. **WALL PUSHUPS:** Players stand 8–11 inches away from a wall. Keeping their legs and body straight, they place their hands against the wall at shoulder height and bend their elbows until their heads touch the wall. Then they push their body away from the wall by straightening their elbows. Repeat up to 20 times.
4. **CHAIR SIT:** Players stand with their backs against a wall and slowly slide down until they are sitting with their legs parallel to the floor. Putting their hands on their thighs, players see how long they can hold that position.
5. **BEANBAG ARM CIRCLES:** Players hold a beanbag in each hand and extend their arms at shoulder height. Keeping their arms straight, they make 10 small arm circles forward and backward, then 10 large arm circles forward and backward.
6. **THEIR CHOICE:** Players do an exercise of their choice for 20 seconds.
7. **INNER-TUBE STRETCHES:** Pairs sit cross-legged on the floor facing one another. Each player holds on to an inner tube with both hands and pulls the tube back for a count of 10, rests, then repeats twice more. Partners seesaw back and forth while singing "Row, Row, Row Your Boat."

Players sit on their chairs and hook an inner tube behind a front leg. Holding on to the chair seat, players put 1 foot inside the inner tube and work against the tube by straightening their leg. Repeat 10 times with each leg. Players stand facing the back of their chair and loop the inner tube behind a back chair leg. Holding the chair back, players put 1 foot inside the tube and pull their ankle backwards as far as they can. Repeat 10 times with each leg. Players double their tube and then, holding it with both hands, try to pull it apart 10 times.

7.

Activity Circuits

Circuits are composed of a variety of exercises or activities presented at different locations. Players do an exercise for 20–30 seconds, then move to a new exercise station at a given signal. Divide the class into small groups so that there are no more than 4–5 players at one station. Activity circuits make good warm-ups and skill review. Play music to keep players motivated.

1. WARM-UP CIRCUIT

Station #1: Players toss beanbags up and catch them with 1 or 2 hands.

Station #2: Players jump on 2 feet back and forth over paper "candles."

Station #3: Players make shapes with a scarf in each hand.

Station #4: Players sit on chairs and lift their knees to the music as though marching.

Station #5: Players crawl under a long clothesline that has been suspended close to the floor. Then they get up and leap back over it.

Station #6: Players balance on a masking-tape line on 1 foot, then on their toes, then with their eyes closed.

Station #7: Players leap over several long cardboard boxes and back.

Station #8: Players spin hoops on any part of their body.

Station #9: Players hit or bounce beach balls against a wall.

Station #10: Players keep a balloon up in the air.

2. BEACH BALL CIRCUIT

Station #1: Players hit beach balls overhand or underhand against a wall.

Station #2: Players bounce a beach ball with their hands, elbows, head, or other part of their body.

Station #3: Players toss a beach ball through a hanging hoop.

Station #4: Players roll beach balls at milk cartons to knock them down.

Station #5: Players toss beach balls into cardboard boxes.

Station #6: Players make up their own trick with a beach ball.

▶ **Hint:** Almost any age or group can do circuit activities. For younger children, keep the circuit short and vary activities.

Obstacle Course

You may want to arrange 2 identical courses so 2 groups can play at once. Players can time how long it takes them to cover the course. Make sure players wait until the player in front is halfway through the course before beginning.

1. FITNESS OBSTACLE COURSE

Obstacle #1: Players weave around milk carton markers.

Obstacle #2: Players crawl under a large box supported on either side by chairs.

Obstacle #3: Players slide from foot to foot sideways between 2 short ropes or pieces of tape.

Obstacle #4: Players leap over a series of short ropes on the ground.

Obstacle #5: Players crawl through a hoop taped to 2 chairs.

Obstacle #6: Players step through a series of hoops.

Obstacle #7: Players roll along a mat.

Obstacle #8: Players leap over several cardboard box hurdles.

Obstacle #9: Players ride a tricycle to the finish line and tag the next player, then return the tricycle to position.

2. CARDBOARD BOX OBSTACLE COURSE

Obstacle #1: Players "skate" (wearing shoe boxes) to a cardboard tunnel.

Obstacle #2: Players crawl through the tunnel.

Obstacle #3: Players jump over box hurdles. (Players who knock down a hurdle must set it up again.)

Obstacle #4: Players push a box to another tunnel. The far end of the tunnel is closed so players crawl into the tunnel, touch the end, and crawl out backwards.

Obstacle #5: Players go back over the obstacles to the starting point.

Olympics

All the students in a class, grade, or school participate in various events as representatives of different countries. Have on hand reference books with pictures of the countries' flags, stick-on name tags, felt-tipped markers, wastebaskets, music, aluminum foil, soda straws, masking-tape, string, newspaper, small bags, peanuts, plastic foam plates, pretzel sticks, lengths of rope, clothespins, and shoe boxes of various sizes.

Begin by having children pick a country to represent. Have them draw their country's flag and print the name on their name tags. Conduct the events in a large room or outdoor field.

1. **SHOT-PUT FOR DISTANCE:** Players hold an aluminum foil ball in the palm of 1 hand level with their ears. At the signal, the players push their shots into the air, extending their arms and not moving their feet.

2. **"HAMMER" THROW:** Stuff a paper bag with a ball of newspaper and tie it with a piece of string 12 inches long. Holding the end of the string, players spin around 3 times, and then let go to see how far their "hammer" will go.

3. **JAVELIN THROW:** Tape one end of soda straws. Students try to throw their straws into a wastebasket goal.

4. **DISCUS THROW:** Tape 2 heavy plastic foam plates together. Holding the "discus" like a flying disk and throwing it out and away from their waists, students try to throw the discus the longest distance.

5. **POLE VAULT:** Players race to eat a pretzel stick.

6. **100-INCH DASH:** Measure 100 inches on the floor or field and mark start and finish lines. At the signal, students try to reach the finish line, moving their feet alternately 1 inch at a time.

7. **STANDING BROAD STRETCH:** With the toes 1 foot behind a line, students see who can take the widest step. They may balance themselves with their hands on the ground.

▶ **Hint:** Players should do this activity slowly and stop if they feel any strain in their groin muscles.

1.

8. FROG HURDLES: Place 6–8 strips of masking tape outside, fasten lengths of rope into the ground with clothespins equal distances apart. At the signal, players hop like frogs (squatting with their hands on the ground between their feet) down the track, over each of the hurdles.

9. PEANUT HOCKEY: On a tabletop (or a flat outdoor surface), players try to make a goal by tapping 3 peanuts with a pencil into a cardboard-box goal. Score 1 point for each goal.

10. FIGURE SKATING: Students step into 2 shoe boxes a little bit larger than their shoes. (Younger children may skate with just 1 box.) Working alone or with partner, students "skate" to the music for 30 seconds, making up routines to fit the mood and rhythm of the music.

▶ **Closing Ceremony:** Representatives from each country shake hands and sit down together to an international banquet (bag lunches from home or a special snack).

9.

Field Day

These events emphasize participation instead of winning. Set up the games for individuals, partners, or teams. Invite school administrators to serve as judges. For these events, you will need soda crackers, paper bags, peanuts, plastic spoons, hard-boiled eggs, cardboard boxes, burlap bags, and balloons.

1. **CRACKER AND WHISTLE RACE:** Give players each 1 soda cracker. At the signal, players eat the crackers and then see who can whistle a tune first.
2. **INCH-BY-INCH RACE:** Players line up with their feet side by side. At the signal, they shuffle each foot 1 inch at a time until they reach a finish line.
3. **SHOE RACE:** All players take off 1 shoe, put it into a pile, and stand at the starting line. At the signal, players run to the pile of shoes, find their shoe and put it on, and run back to the finish line.
4. **POP-A-BAG RACE:** Give players each 1 small paper bag. At the signal, players race to a marker, blow up their bags and pop them with their hands, and race back to the finish line.
5. **OUTDOOR ROLLING RACE:** Players wearing old clothes and long-sleeved shirts roll down a hill or incline to see who can reach the bottom first.
▶ **Hint:** Make sure the field is dry and that rolling players are far enough apart.

3.

6. **PEANUT SPOON DRIBBLE:** Players use a plastic spoon to dribble a peanut to a finish line, around a marker, and back.
7. **HARD-BOILED EGG RACE:** Balancing a hard-boiled egg on their spoon, players walk to a finish line, around a marker, and back. Players may pick up and replace any egg that falls off. Players use 1 hand only and may not place their thumb on the egg.
8. **HURDLE RACE:** Arrange cardboard boxes lengthwise in several lines. Players jump over the boxes, run around a marker, and return to the finish line.
9. **BAG RACE:** Give each player a burlap bag to stand in. Holding the bag up to their waist with both hands, players jump to the finish line. The object is to see who can jump all the way to the finish line without falling.
10. **OUTDOOR WATER BALLOON PARTNER TOSS:** Partners face one another, 1 player holding a small balloon half filled with water. At the signal, partners toss the balloon back and forth without breaking it. After each catch, partners each take 1 step backwards. The object is to see which pair can stand farthest apart and still catch the water balloon without breaking it.

Relay Races

Teams of players will enjoy these races. Equipment includes shoe boxes, hoops or tires, string, balloons, tin cans, yarn or sock balls, paper plates, marbles, small bowls, sponges, soda bottles, and markers. Have all players sit down when the last player on their team crosses the finish line.

1. **SHOE BOX RACE:** Wearing a shoe box on each foot, players race down the course, around a marker, and back. They then hand the shoe boxes to the next players to wear.
2. **ROLL RACE:** Players roll a hoop or tire with their hands down and back.
3. **BAT-THE-BALLOON RACE:** Players bat a balloon down the course and back.
▶ **Hint:** If you are playing outdoors, tie a string on each balloon and have players run with them around the marker and back.
4. **BEACH BALL CIRCLE BOUNCE:** Teams sit in a circle on chairs. At the signal, the first player bounces the beach ball to the next player to the left, and so on, until the ball reaches the last player. If you are playing outside, players can bounce the ball with both hands as they run to a marker and back.

2.

5. KICK-THE-CANS RACE: Each player kicks 2 tin cans down and back.

6. YARN BALL RACE: Players stand in line behind one another with their feet about a shoulder width apart. At the signal, the first player bends over and rolls a yarn or sock ball through his or her legs and through the tunnel formed by the legs of all the teammates. If the ball stops midway, the nearest player continues to roll the ball until it reaches the end of the line.

7. MARBLE PLATE RACE: Teams line up one behind the other. The first player of each team holds a sturdy paper plate with 5 marbles on it. At the signal, the player passes the plate between his or her legs to the next player, and so on, until the plate reaches the last person. If any marbles drop off, players must replace them before continuing to pass the plate back.

8. SPONGE AND BOTTLE RACE: Each team has a small bowl of water and a sponge. The first player soaks the sponge with water and races with it to an empty soda bottle. The player squeezes as much water as possible into the bottle and then runs back to give the sponge to the next player. Teams try to fill up their bottles first.

▶ **Hint:** This outdoor game is especially good on a hot day. Other relay races that appear in Part One are Cardboard Squares Partner Race, Paper Balls Over/Under Relay, and Team Chair Relay.

Tag Games

For all these games, instruct children to tag gently, with 1 hand only, on players' arms or shoulders. If your playing area is small, divide the class into groups and rotate them often. For faster action, have more than one It. Children who are It can wear colored vests. Other equipment includes lengths of rope, balloons, carpet squares, paper balls, and yarn or sock balls.

1. **ROPE BALANCE TAG:** Lay out short rope for each player around the playing area. It tries to tag any player who is not standing and balancing on a rope.
2. **BALLOON-IN-THE-AIR TAG:** As It hits a large balloon into the air, the other players scatter. It tries to tag player before the balloon hits the floor. If It does not tag another player, then he or she is It for another round.
3. **CARPET SQUARE TAG:** Scatter 1 carpet square for each player around the playing area. It tries to tag any player who is not sitting on a carpet square and pretending to pedal a bicycle.

4. PAPER BALL TAG: It kicks a paper ball around a playing area, trying to hit another player's feet with the ball.

5. PENNY TEAM TAG: Give 1 player on each team a penny. Each team goes into a huddle, and the leader secretly gives the penny to another team member. At the signal, players try to tag members of the other team. A player who is tagged opens his or her hands to show if he or she has the penny. The object is to be the first team to find the other team's penny.

6. SNOWBALL TAG: Players tag with yarn or sock balls instead of their hands. Place yarn balls on a middle line of the playing area. At the signal, the players from both teams run to the center, pick up 1 ball each, and return to the team throwing line. From there, they try to throw the balls at the feet of the other team's players. Any player who is hit on the feet crosses the center line and becomes a member of the other team. After 30 seconds, the leader blows the whistle and counts the number of players on each side. The object is for each team to get the most players on its side. Players then return to their original team, the leader replaces the balls on the center line, and play continues for 2 more rounds.

▶ **Hints:** Discourage ball hogs by reminding players to pick up only 1 ball at a time. Direct players to throw only at the feet of the other team. This is a strenuous game and a good warm-up.

6.

Birthday Games

In addition to these games that are appropriate for birthday fun, see also Birthday Exchange in the section Games That Use Sheets. These games call for animal cookies, a pillowcase, classroom objects, treasure maps, treasure bags, balloons, and music.

1. **ANIMAL COOKIES:** The leader passes out 1–2 animal-shaped cookies to each player in a circle. The players secretly look at them. Each player in turn then describes the animal or imitates its sound so the other players can guess the animal. At the end of the game, everyone eats the animal cookies.

2. **PILLOWCASE GUESS:** Place several items into a pillowcase and pass it around the circle to each player, who feels the objects with his or her hands. When everyone has had a turn, players guess what the objects are.

3. **TREASURE HUNT:** Give each group a treasure map with picture clues and/or written directions. Each group follows the directions to find its own small bag of treasure (foil-covered chocolate or gum coins).

4. **MUSICAL BALLOONS:** Give each pair 1 large balloon. Players hold the balloon between them (on their backs, foreheads, shoulders, or other part of their bodies) without using their hands. When the music starts, players dance to the music without letting the balloons drop.

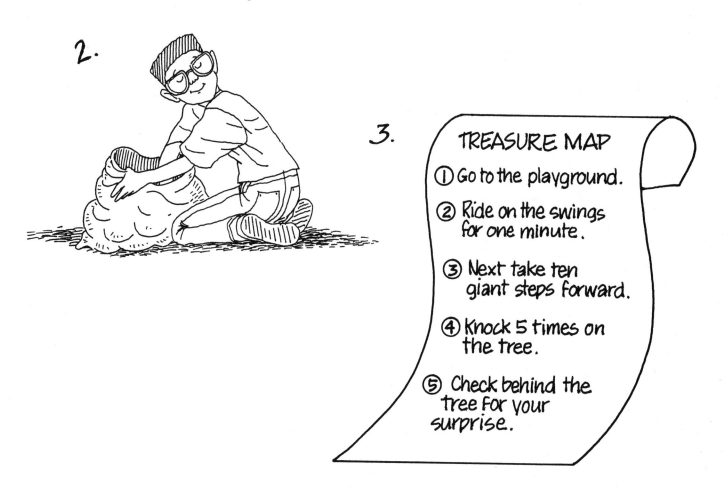

2.

3.

TREASURE MAP
1 Go to the playground.
2 Ride on the swings for one minute.
3 Next take ten giant steps forward.
4 Knock 5 times on the tree.
5 Check behind the tree for your surprise.

Holiday and Seasonal Games

These games add fun to celebrations of special days. You will need brooms, a large sheet, construction paper, double-sided tape, cardboard, tissue paper, dustpans, brushes, and table tennis balls.

Halloween

1. BROOMSTICK RELAY: The first player on each team straddles a broom, races down the course to a marker, and back. The player gives the broom to the next player and goes to the end of the line.

2. WHO'S THE GHOST?: Players sit with a sheet draped over them. It taps a player and asks, "Who is the ghost?" The player answers, "I am the ghost." It has 2 guesses to identify the player.

Thanksgiving

3. GOBBLE, GOBBLE, GOBBLE: It sits with his or her back to the rest of the players. The leader points to a player who says, "Gobble, Gobble, Gobble." It has 2 chances to guess the gobbler. If It does not guess the gobbler, he or she becomes It.

Winter

4. PIN ON SANTA'S TOY SACK: Attach a large picture of Santa to a wall. Give each player a small paper toy sack backed with a piece of double-sided tape. Each player in turn is blindfolded and tries to pin the toy sack on Santa's back.

5. JUMP THE HANUKKAH CANDLES: Arrange 2 sets of 8 folded construction-paper candles around the playing area. The first player on each team tries to jump over all the candles without knocking any over. The player runs back to the front of the line, tags the next player, and goes to the end of the line.

Valentine's Day

6. VALENTINE TAG: Give players on 2 teams names of items that are related to Valentine's Day: Cupid, arrow, bow, heart, etc. It stands between the 2 teams lined up facing each other. At the signal, It calls out 1 or more names. Players try to run across to the other team before It tags them. Anyone who is tagged becomes It's valentine and tries to help It tag more players.

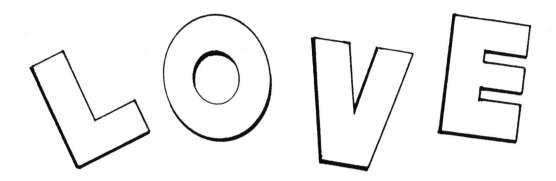

7. L-O-V-E SEARCH: Scatter several sets of the cardboard letters L,O,V,E around the playing area. At the signal, teams or pairs try to gather, in order, as many sets as they can. Players can also trade letters.

Spring
8. MARCH WIND RACE: Give each player on 2 or more relay teams 1 paper fan made of folded construction paper and 5 small tissue-paper balls. At the signal, the first player on each team uses the fan to blow the balls into the team's goal box at the far end of the playing area. The player then runs back to tag the next player. Teams see how long it takes to get all the balls into the goal.

9. SPRING CLEANING RACE: Place wastebaskets in front of 2 or more relay teams. At the signal, the first player on each team takes a dustpan and brush and runs to the table tennis balls at the far end of the playing area. He or she sweeps 1 ball into the pan and runs back to put it into the wastebasket. Then the next player takes the dustpan and brush. Teams see how many balls they can clean up.

8.

Carnival

A carnival is a good way to raise money or just have fun. Older children can help younger children design, build, and run booths. These activities are offered as suggestions. Your class will probably come up with many more ideas.

1. **FISHING POND:** Drape a sheet over a clothesline. Players take turns "fishing" for small prizes with a fishing pole that has a snap clothespin tied onto the line.
2. **ODDS N' ENDS BOOTH:** Collect white elephants, secondhand books, and so forth. Offer them for sale for real or play money.
3. **FOOD BOOTH:** Offer simple ethnic foods or giant chocolate chip cookies (baked as a project) and lemonade.
4. **PENNY PITCH:** Place small prizes on a large sheet of cardboard divided into squares. Players pitch pennies into the squares to win the prizes. Pennies must land completely inside the squares.
5. **FACE PAINTING:** Use nontoxic face paints to draw designs on players' faces or the backs of their hands.
6. **BURIED TREASURE:** Bury small prizes in a container of sand and give players small toy shovels.
7. **FOOTBALL TOSS:** Players get 3 chances to toss a sponge football through a spinning hoop.

8. CUPCAKE PAN BOUNCE: Give players 3 tries to bounce table tennis balls into the compartments of a cupcake pan.

9. WASTEBASKET BOUNCE: Give players 3 tries to bounce a basketball into a wastebasket.

10. PIN-THE-HAT-ON-THE-CELEBRITY: Hang a poster of a famous person on a wall. Make a paper hat the celebrity might wear, and attach double-sided tape to the back. Blindfolded players try to place the hat as close as they can to the celebrity's head.

11. SINK-A-BOAT: Float several small boats in a pan of water. Give 2–3 players water pistols. At the signal, players stand behind a line and try to sink a boat by squirting water at it.

8.

Swim Meet

Conduct these games in the shallow (waist-deep) end of a pool. There should be a certified lifeguard on duty. Non-swimmers and differently abled children should wear flotation vests or jackets.

1. **APPLE PUSH RACE:** Each swimmer pushes a floating apple across a pool with his or her chin.
2. **FLOTATION RACE:** Each swimmer sits on an inner tube or other flotation device and paddles across the pool.
3. **FLUTTER KICK RACE:** Each swimmer holds on with both hands to a plastic bottle or kick board. Float various objects (plastic toys, clothespins, etc.) in the playing area. At the signal, teams try to gather as many floating objects as possible and put them in their washbasket.
5. **BEACH BALL BALANCE:** Each player has a medium-sized beach ball. At the signal, players try to push the beach ball under water and sit on it by wrapping their legs around it. Players see who can balance on the beach ball the longest.
6. **PLASTIC BOTTLE:** It holds the handle of a plastic bottle while trying to tag another player. Players who duck their head under water are "safe" and cannot be tagged. The player It tags becomes It for the next round.
7. **KEEP AWAY:** Anchor a plastic bottle to the bottom of the pool by tying it to a rubber brick with a length of plastic rope. Players hold hands in a circle around the anchored carton. Players try to pull each other into the center of the circle to touch the bottle. Whoever touches the bottle leaves the first circle and forms another circle around another bottle.
8. **DROP THE BOTTLE:** Players hold hands in a circle while It walks or swims behind them holding a plastic bottle. When It drops the bottle behind a player, he or she turns around, takes the carton, and tries to tag It. It tries to walk or swim around the circle to the empty place. The second player now becomes It.
9. **SWIMMING SUPPORTS RACE:** For each player, tie 2 plastic bottles together with plastic line. Swimmers place the supports under their shoulders as they back-stroke across the pool. Repeat, with swimmers paddling and then placing the supports under their feet.

9.

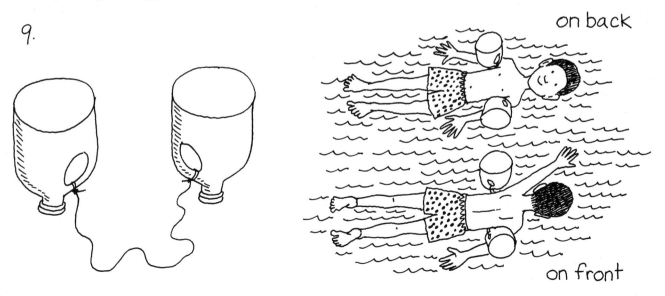

on back

on front

PART THREE

Making and Adapting Equipment

Making and Adapting Equipment

Before you go out to buy supplies, tap your class resources. Send home the Letter to Parents on page 11 and ask for the materials you need. If you must go to outside sources, look in discount stores, thrift shops, garage sales, outlets, and recycling centers as well as in hardware stores, educational supply stores, craft shops, and fabric stores. Parent volunteers may be willing to make some of the following equipment for the class.

Beanbags

Use small (4–5 inch) or large (6–8 inch) squares of scrap material. Double-stitch the seams, leaving 2 inches open along one side. Turn the bag inside out, push out the corners with a darning needle, and fill it with dried beans or packing beads. Hand- or machine-stitch closed.

Beanbag Targets

Take 3 squares (3 x 3 feet or larger) of cardboard or scrap wood and hinge them together with tape or small hinges. On one side, draw a clown face and cut out eyes, nose, and mouth. The shapes and sizes of the holes depend on the age of the players and how difficult you want the game to be. On another side, draw a Tick, Tack, Toe game with holes cut out in each square. On the third side, draw or paint a game of your choice.

side view

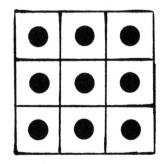

clown target

tic-tack-toe target

Plastic Bottle Markers and Catchers

Collect plastic gallon or quart bottles from milk, juice, bleach, etc. Remove the labels, rinse thoroughly, and let dry. For markers, weight the bottles with sand, water, or pebbles. For catchers, cut as shown and tape edges to prevent injuries.

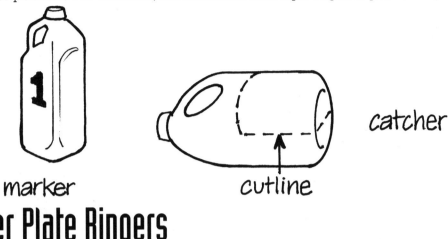

marker   cutline   catcher

Paper Plate Ringers

Use a craft knife or sharp scissors to cut out the centers of study paper plates, leaving only the outside ring. Reinforce by taping with masking-tape or tape lightweight cardboard rings to the plate rings.

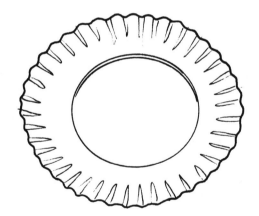

Flying Disks

Face 2 sturdy paper or plastic foam plates together. Tape around the edges with masking tape.

tape

Paper Tube Hummers

Take a double thickness of wax paper and cover 1 end of a paper tube. Secure it with a rubber band or masking tape. Punch a hole near the top of the tube behind the rubber band or tape and another one on the opposite side of the tube. Have players hum into the uncovered end of the tube.

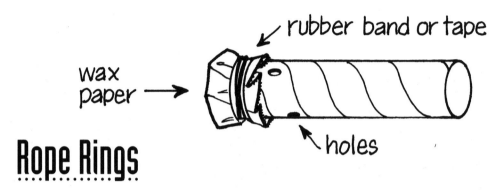

Rope Rings

Use a length of thick, heavy rope or a double thickness of clothesline. Tape the ends with masking tape or electrical tape. Outside, players toss rings at cut-off broomsticks hammered into the ground. Inside, use weighted plastic bottles as targets. You can also insert cut-off broomsticks into several thick squares of plastic foam that you tape to the floor to prevent tipping.

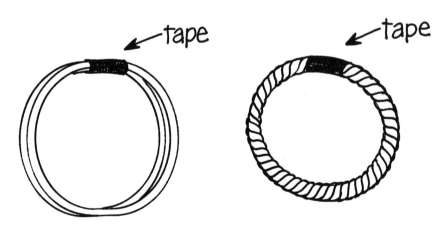

Hoops

Take a length of 1/2-inch plastic tubing plumber's pipe. Insert a 1/2-inch wooden dowel 3 1/2 inches long into both ends of the pipe. Tape the connection several times to secure.

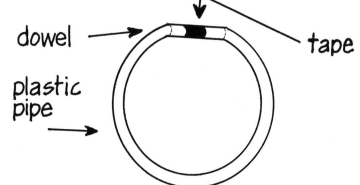

Round Yarn Balls

Crumble a small piece of paper and tape it into a small ball. Tape one end of the yarn to the paper ball and wind it around the ball in different directions until the yarn ball is the desired size. Cut the yarn and use a long craft needle to push the end through the ball to the other side. Knot the end to one of the yarn strands.

Fuzzy Yarn Ball

Take a length of yarn and wrap it about 30 times around a cardboard rectangle 6 inches wide x 8 inches long. Cut the yarn and slip the yarn loops off the cardboard. Tie the loops together in the center with strong string. Repeat, making another bundle of loops. Take both groups of loops and tie them to one another. Then cut the loops in half and spread out the yarn ends. Clip uneven ends for a rounder surface.

Sock Balls

Fold 1 large man's sock, turn the sock inside out, folding in the rest of the sock to make a ball. For a thicker ball, use 2 or more socks.

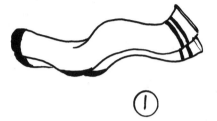  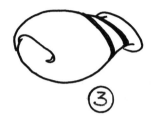

Felt Target Boards

Make a cardboard target board. Glue on felt or flannel.
Use Velcro adhesive balls with the target board.

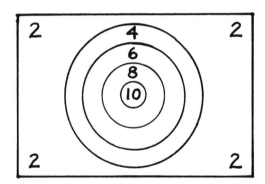

Velcro Adhesive Balls

Glue 5 1 1/2-inch strips of Velcro tape to each table tennis ball. Balls will "stick" to felt—or flannel—covered target boards.

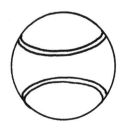  ← Velcro adhesive strips